Willa Cather: A Critical Introduction

WILLA CATHER

A CRITICAL INTRODUCTION

DAVID DAICHES

Professor of English in Cornell University

GREENWOOD PRESS, PUBLISHERS
WESTPORT, CONNECTICUT

Daiches, David, 1912–
 Willa Cather; a critical introduction Westport, Conn.,
Greenwood Press ₁1971, ᶜ1951₁

 vi, 193 p. 23 cm.

 1. Cather, Willa Sibert, 1873–1947.

PS3505.A87Z62 1971   813'.5'2   71–136061
ISBN 0–8371–5211–9   MARC

Library of Congress   71 ₁4₁

Preface

THIS BOOK was written in an attempt to answer the question: "What do you think of the work of Willa Cather?" I am no expert in American literature and have not attempted to give my answer in terms of movements or backgrounds. I have written my reasoned opinion of the novels in chronological order and followed this with some discussion of Miss Cather's poetry and critical writing, in the hope that my critical analyses and appraisals will increase perception and appreciation on the part of both the general reader and the serious student of Miss Cather's work. I have dealt with the novels one by one because I am interested in them as individual literary works rather than as expressions of a philosophy or a point of view. I have not begun by a general discussion of Miss Cather's views and their development, because she is interesting to me as a novelist rather than as a thinker, and her views are worth careful consideration only insofar as they are bound up with the structure and emotional pattern of the novels. In other words, I have tried to write a work of literary criticism and appreciation, not a work of philosophy or *Kulturgeschichte*.

Preface

I should like to express my warm gratitude to Alfred A. Knopf, publisher of *Willa Cather on Writing, One of Ours, A Lost Lady, The Professor's House, Death Comes for the Archbishop, Shadows on the Rock, Youth and the Bright Medusa, Obscure Destinies, Not under Forty,* and *April Twilights and Other Poems,* for permission to quote from these books, and to render similar acknowledgment to the Houghton Mifflin Company, who published *Alexander's Bridge, O Pioneers!, The Song of the Lark,* and *My Ántonia.*

D.D.

October, 1950

Contents

Willa Cather: A Critical Introduction

CHAPTER 1

Apprenticeship

WILLA CATHER was born near Winchester, Virginia, probably in 1874.[1] In 1882 she moved with her parents to a farm near Red Cloud, Nebraska, where she lived until she entered the preparatory school of the University of Nebraska at Lincoln in September, 1890. Her education up to this point had been largely informal, but effective. Her maternal aunt had been a schoolteacher near Winchester, and her mother and grandmother seem to have been well read in the Bible and the classics. She apparently acquired from them a sound introduction to English literature and its background, and when she arrived at Lincoln she was qualified to take her place at once as a girl of literary knowledge and ambitions.

[1] Oddly enough, the year of Miss Cather's birth cannot be absolutely determined, since, presumably as a result of an oversight on her parents' part, it seems never to have been reported and was certainly not recorded. The year of her birth was given as 1875 in *Who's Who in America* until the issue of 1920–1921, when it was changed to 1876. But Mr. W. W. Glass, the Archivist of Winchester, Virginia, having thoroughly searched the record, decided on the available evidence that 1874 must be the proper date; and this is accepted by Dr. James R. Shively, who has carefully investigated Willa Cather's early years.

Willa Cather

Her literary ambitions were clear from the beginning. There is a story of her as a small child in Virginia standing on the footbridge which crossed a stream near her home and reciting Longfellow's poem, "The Bridge." At Lincoln she entered on her literary pursuits with vigor and determination. After her preliminary work at the Latin School she embarked on a four-year program at the University which concentrated on English literature, with considerable work in Latin, Greek, and French, and courses in German, rhetoric, history, philosophy, and journalism. At the same time she threw herself into extracurricular literary activities with an energy which impressed and sometimes exasperated her contemporaries. She joined the Union Literary Society of which she became secretary, appeared in the productions of the University Dramatic Club, wrote for and edited the *Hesperian,* a student magazine which appeared fortnightly, and in 1894 edited *Sombrero,* the senior year book. In her last two years at College she also wrote dramatic criticism and fugitive pieces for the *Nebraska State Journal.*

At Lincoln Miss Cather dressed in a masculine way, had her hair cut short, and made it clear that she had a good opinion of herself and was going to become an important writer. It was during her college years that she learned to admire William Jennings Bryan, then at Lincoln, whose influence on her later political thinking is to be seen in many of her novels and short stories. The Populist movement, arising out of the exhaustion of free land in the West and the increasingly precarious position of the farmer in a competitive industrial

2

economy, left a permanent trace on Miss Cather's thinking: acting on her own knowledge of western farming life it led her more and more to look back on the pioneering days as the period of America's lost glory and to regard commercial and industrial progress with suspicion. We shall see later how this is reflected in her fiction, and how in some respects it defined the direction of her progress as a novelist.

Of the writing that Miss Cather did in her student days, the dramatic criticism is probably the most mature. Her comments on plays and actors show a sophistication and an assurance which are not as a rule displayed by the stories she wrote for the *Hesperian*. They are not profound, nor do they exhibit any considerable critical originality, but they are shrewd and perceptive and show how quickly she made herself at home in the world of art. Her early stories, if more uneven than her early dramatic criticism, are, nevertheless, more interesting, since they show her using themes she was to exploit later with considerable success.

One of the most interesting of her *Hesperian* pieces is a grim little story entitled "Peter," telling of the last days of a Czech immigrant. Peter Sadelack, once a second violinist in the great theatre at Prague, had lost his job as a result of a stroke of paralysis "which made his arms so weak that his bowing was uncertain." He emigrated to the United States and took up a homestead in southwestern Nebraska. A shiftless man of artistic temperament, he was unable to adjust to life in the New World and was persecuted by his thrifty and mean-spirited son to the point where he committed suicide. The story centers on the final crisis between Peter and his son: the son has insisted that Peter sell his old violin, for he needs the money, and Peter feels he would rather die than give up his last relic of his earlier and happier life. A flash back fills in the story of Peter's life in Prague; and then we return to the present and the suicide scene—a scene which Willa Cather was to employ later with little change in her account of the suicide of Mr. Shimerda in *My Antonia*.

"Peter" contains the germ of much of Miss Cather's later writing. The elderly and sensitive immigrant who is unable to adjust to the pioneering life appears in several of her early novels and illustrates that interest in the relation between the Old World and the New which runs right through her work. The conflict between the generations—the hard and thrifty son, the romantic and dreamy father—is another important theme in her novels; it is a theme which Miss Cather later linked to her presentation of the decline of a pioneering civilization and the intrusion of a commercial world into a once heroic society. This again can be related to her interest in the Populist movement and her resentment at what the financial East had done to the Western farmer. "Peter" is a crude and even melodramatic piece; but it has a straightforwardness of style, a quiet intensity in the telling, which promise well. The concluding paragraph, with its desperate attempt at restraint, indicates her stylistic ideal:

In the morning Antone found him stiff, frozen fast in a pool of blood. They could not straighten him out enough to fit a coffin, so they buried him in a pine box. Before the funeral Antone carried to town the fiddlebow which Peter had forgotten to break. Antone was very thrifty, and a better man than his father had been.[2]

Beside the Nebraska sketches are more exotic pieces, such as "A Tale of the White Pyramid," set in ancient Egypt, or "A Night at Greenway Court," an eighteenth-century tale involving feuds, kings, and codes of honor. These are in the minority, however, and Miss Cather seems to have preferred grim little tales of simple farming folk caught up in some monstrous tragedy of maladjustment or injustice. "The Clemency of the Court," for example, tells with fierce irony of a simple son of Russian immigrants who was driven to commit an innocent murder and, having been sentenced to life imprisonment, was tortured to death by prison guards. The political overtones here are quite distinct.

There are silly and pretentious pieces among those Miss Cather wrote for the *Hesperian,* which would be of no interest at all if we did not know what their author was later to become. These at least show her experimenting with different styles. The style she cultivated most successfully at this stage, however, was the deliberately simple one of "Peter," in which restraint is employed in order to achieve ironical overtones. Structurally, she had already discovered the flash back, which was to remain a favorite device throughout her career as a writer of fiction.

Her sense of the pioneering life, her knowledge of farming in the Midwest, her acquaintance with the dif-

[2] *Writings from Willa Cather's Campus Years,* ed. James R. Shively (Lincoln: University of Nebraska Press, 1950), p. 45.

ferent kinds of immigrants who had settled in Nebraska
—Czechs, Swedes, Norwegians, Germans, Russians—
gave her abundant material to work with, while her
reading, her literary ambitions, her awareness of the
great world of art and culture awaiting her in the East,
turned her thoughts to experiments in style and form,
suggested kinds of preciousness and aesthetic self-
assertiveness, turning her away sometimes from the
material she had ready to hand to more obviously
"literary" themes and attitudes. The conflict between
what might be called the emotional base of her art and
her self-consciousness as an artist is to be seen throughout her early work. Her first short stories to be published
in book form were not about Nebraska farmers but
about artists, their problems, their special kind of sensibility, and their place in the world. And her first novel,
as we shall see, was set in Boston and London, and its
characters moved in a Jamesian world.

After her graduation at the University of Nebraska
in 1895, Miss Cather became a member of the staff of the
Lincoln *Courier,* working as associate editor until the
end of the year, when she left for Pittsburgh, thus closing
the Nebraska chapter of her life. At Pittsburgh she
worked for the *Leader* and then (from 1901) taught as
head of the English Department of the Allegheny High
School. She spent summers in Nebraska, Colorado, and
Wyoming; she made trips to Europe; she wrote poems
and short stories which she contributed to *Cosmopoli-
tan, McClure's Magazine, Lippincott's Magazine,* and
other periodicals. In 1903 she published a volume of her
verse under the title *April Twilights,* and in 1905

McClure, Philipps and Company brought out *The Troll Garden,* her first volume of short stories.

Of Willa Cather's poetry, which is of no great significance, we shall speak briefly in the final chapter. *The Troll Garden,* which also will be discussed later, Willa Cather herself came to regard as among her juvenilia and refused to have it reprinted as a complete book, though the stories in it which she wished to preserve were included in *Youth and the Bright Medusa,* published in 1920. Both these volumes of short stories deal with the artist's life. The stories of *The Troll Garden* were Willa Cather's claim to be made free of the world of art, and they show an almost feverish attempt to demonstrate that she was at home in that world and knew both its glories and its dangers.

Her attack on the world of art was also made directly, by extending her acquaintance with literary and musical circles in New York and elsewhere. In 1906 S. S. McClure, impressed by her stories, offered her a position on his magazine. She moved to New York on accepting this position; two years later she was made managing editor, and her position as a literary figure if not yet as a distinguished writer was assured.

Between 1908 and 1911, the period during which she held the position of managing editor of *McClure's Magazine,* she traveled a great deal in Europe and in the southwestern states and became more and more at home in both the European and the American world of art, letters, and music. Music had been one of her passions since childhood. While at Lincoln she had made excursions to Omaha and Chicago to see operas and plays, and once in the East she eagerly seized the opportunity of enlarging her knowledge of music and drama and especially of opera. Later, when on one of her south-western trips she discovered Gertrude Hall's *The Wagnerian Romances,* her interest in Wagnerian opera, already great, developed into a permanent enthusiasm, an enthusiasm based on thorough knowledge and under-standing of the Wagnerian art form: this was to show in her novel, *The Song of the Lark,* and is visible in a great deal of her subsequent work.

In 1911 Miss Cather resigned her position with *McClure's* to devote all her time to independent writ-ing. For all her fierce ambition to be a writer, it was thus relatively late in life that she settled down to devote her-self entirely to her own fiction. In 1912 her first novel, *Alexander's Bridge,* was published in Boston by Hough-ton Mifflin.

CHAPTER 2

Early Novels

Alexander's Bridge, Willa Cather's first novel, is in a sense a mere literary exercise. Deftly constructed, written with a sensitive precision (learned from Henry James), full of warmly imagined interiors, and containing some fine set descriptions, it nevertheless fails in that the central emotional situations are never fully realized. It is the story of a successful Boston engineer and bridge designer verging on middle age who, on a trip to London on business, meets the girl with whom, many years before, during his romantic youth in Paris, he had had a brief but passionate love affair. Happily married to a devoted and beautiful wife, he is nevertheless awakened by this encounter with his first love (now a successful actress) to a fierce renewal of his youth, and this struggle between ebbing youth and oncoming middle age is the real theme of the novel. The actress is still in love with him and has cherished his memory from their early Paris days, and on his frequent trips to London he becomes more and more involved, against his will and with a sense of discomfort and almost of despair. The position becomes ever more complex and the problem insoluble:

he realizes that, as he put it to Hilda, the actress, "I am not a man who can live two lives: each life spoils the other." His death, caused by the collapse of an unfinished bridge, solves the problem, and both Hilda and his wife Winifred remain to cherish, each in her own way, the memory of the Alexander they loved.

The novel is not centered on Bartley Alexander's relations with the two women, but on Bartley Alexander himself, who remains continually in the foreground, a character never fully explained, symbol of successful energy which is, nevertheless, not wholly contented with itself. Miss Cather seems fascinated, and a little mystified, by her character. Instead of presenting to the reader someone whom, having created, she fully understands, she seems rather to be exploring him along with the reader and to know no more of him than each successive incident in the story reveals. Is this merely the study of a man at the "dangerous age" of forty when he is liable to break out into some new kind of emotional life? Miss Cather was clearly interested in this phenomenon, for in later novels she has other male characters similarly break loose at the same age. But the book is not organized in order to illuminate this kind of situation. It is organized, one might say, for the sake of organization, and the neat disposal of the problem by Alexander's opportune death just before he commits himself is no real resolution of the plot but rather the solution by fictional artifice of what has not been solved by the life generated in the novel itself.

The novel is carefully enclosed within brackets, as it were. It opens with a description of the visit of Professor

Lucius Wilson, elderly "Professor of Philosophy in a Western university" to the Alexanders' home in Boston. Professor Wilson had taught Alexander as a student. At the end of the book Wilson, now retired, has settled in London and is talking with Hilda about the dead Alexander in a conversation which parallels his opening discussion of Alexander with his wife Winifred. Wilson makes other occasional appearances throughout the novel, and his purpose seems to be to provide a vantage point from which Alexander's situation can be observed. He is a mild, self-effacing man, perfectly suited for the part of the sympathetic observer. But in the body of the book he appears only occasionally and for no particular reason: the main action is described directly without the intervention of the observer; and the reader feels that Wilson has been introduced to provide a perspective which is not in fact employed. There is, indeed, no very clear perspective in the book. Many of the finest passages are descriptions of interiors or of street sights and sounds: these passages, though memorable in their way and constituting what remains in the reader's mind as the flavor of the novel long after he has read it, are not always properly associated with the emotional situation to which they should be giving added richness. They remain apart, as workmanlike pieces of prose without any organic function within the novel.

The opening description of Professor Wilson approaching the Alexanders' house in Brimmer Street, Boston, is a fine set piece:

. . . Wilson was standing quite still, contemplating with a whimsical smile the slanting street, with its worn paving, its irregular, gravely colored houses, and the row of naked trees on which the thin sunlight was still shining. The gleam of the river at the foot of the hill made him blink a little, not so much because it was too bright as because he found it so pleasant. The few passers-by glanced at him unconcernedly, and even the children who hurried along with their school-bags under their arms seemed to find it perfectly natural that a tall brown gentleman should be standing there, looking up through his glasses at the gray housetops.

The sun sank rapidly; the silvery light had faded from the bare boughs and the watery twilight was setting in when Wilson at last walked down the hill, descending into cooler and cooler depths of grayish shadow. His nostril, long unused to it, was quick to detect the smell of wood smoke in the air, blended with the odor of moist spring earth and the saltiness that came up the river with the tide. He crossed Charles Street between jangling street cars and shelving lumber drays, and after a moment of uncertainty wound into Brimmer Street. The street was quite deserted, and hung with a thin bluish haze.

This is good descriptive prose, in spite of a certain monotony of the rhythms of the sentence-endings ("on which the thin sunlight was still shining"; "looking up through his glasses at the gray housetops"; "cooler and cooler depths of grayish shadow"; "deserted, and hung with a thin, bluish haze"). Throughout the book there are many passages of this kind, set in both Boston and London.

It is in the conversation between Wilson and Winifred, and later between Wilson, Winifred, and Alexander, that the main theme of the book is set going, with a curious and rather artificial deliberateness. Wilson is talking to Alexander:

"Yet I always used to feel that there was a weak spot where some day strain would tell. Even after you began to climb, I stood down in the crowd and watched you with— well, not with confidence. The more dazzling the front you presented, the higher your façade rose, the more I expected to see a big crack zigzagging from top to bottom,"—he indicated its course in the air with his forefinger,—"then a crash and clouds of dust. It was curious. I had such a clear picture of it."

Or, again Wilson talking to Alexander:

"You've changed. You have decided to leave some birds in the bushes. You used to want them all."

Alexander's chair creaked. "I still want a good many," he said rather gloomily.

The expected crack does eventually appear (though we are told later, when the bridge collapses and kills Alexander, that "even Lucius Wilson did not see in this accident the disaster he had once foretold"), and Alexander does go after one of the birds he had earlier decided to leave in the bushes. This is all very neat and tidy, but it has no real substance. Wilson's analysis of Alexander's character has no adequate meaning for us; we do not understand why he expected a big crack to appear in the façade; we do not even fully understand why Alexander should be speaking "rather gloomily" when he replies to Wilson. The characters are not fully realized.

But in its way the novel is skillful. It has a beautifully

clean surface, the dialogue moving along with a calm
ease and each phase of the action being presented with a
quiet assurance. If it lacks what Henry James called
"the sense of felt life" it possesses, on the other hand,
something of the adroitness, even the brilliance, of an
exercise—or, to use a musical analogy which Miss
Cather would have appreciated, of an *étude;* but it
never quite becomes a "piece."

Willa Cather felt this herself. In a preface written in
1922 for a new edition of the novel she was able to speak
from the vantage point of her full self-discovery as a
novelist. "The writer, at the beginning of his career, is
often more interested in his discoveries about his art
than in the homely truths which have been about him
from his cradle." And very properly, too, we might add.
It was a good sign that Miss Cather began her career as a
novelist by demonstrating an interest in the craft of
fiction rather than by slopping on to paper her more
immediate autobiographical impulses. Her experience
with a completely objective art, however imperfectly
realized, made it all the more likely that she would be
able to use her autobiographical impulses successfully
when she came to handle them. "Back in the files of the
College magazine, there were once several of my perfectly honest but very clumsy attempts to give the story
of some of the Scandinavians and Bohemian settlers who
lived not far from my father's farm," she once told an
interviewer. "These early stories were bald, clumsy, and
emotional." She was wise enough to start her serious
career as a novelist from a completely different angle and
not repeat the "bald, clumsy, and emotional" experi-

ments of her youth. *Alexander's Bridge* may not be a very good novel, but, in spite of Willa Cather's later opinion to the contrary, it was the right kind of first novel for a novelist to write.

In her preface to the 1922 edition of *Alexander's Bridge* Willa Cather felt it necessary to explain that *"Alexander's Bridge* was my first novel, and does not deal with the kind of subject-matter in which I now find myself at home." It was written in 1911, and her second novel, *O Pioneers!*, was written the following year. "The difference in quality in the two books is an illustration of the fact that it is not always easy for the inexperienced writer to distinguish between his own material and that which he would like to make his own." The subject she now considered as "her own" was pioneering in Nebraska, the state she knew so well. Returning from Europe soon after the publication of *Alexander's Bridge* she went for six months to Arizona and New Mexico:

The longer I stayed in a country I really did care about, and among people who were a part of the country, the more unnecessary and superficial a book like *Alexander's Bridge* seemed to me. . . .

When I got back to Pittsburgh I began to write a book entirely for myself; a story about some Scandinavians and Bohemians who had been neighbors of ours when I lived on a ranch in Nebraska, when I was eight or nine years old. . . . Here there was no arranging or "inventing"; everything was spontaneous and took its own place, right or wrong.[1]

[1] "My First Novels," in *Willa Cather on Writing* (New York: Knopf, 1949), reprinted from *The Colophon* (Part 6, 1931).

In thus changing her course, and returning to themes she had treated in her undergraduate writing, Miss Cather was acting on the advice of Sarah Orne Jewett, who encouraged her to "give herself up to the pleasure of recapturing in memory people and places [she] had believed forgotten." In her preface to her selection of Miss Jewett's short stories (1925) she quoted an observation from one of Miss Jewett's letters: "*The thing that teases the mind over and over for years, and at last gets itself put down rightly on paper—whether little or great, it belongs to Literature.*" So in *O Pioneers!* she surrendered to what had been teasing her mind over and over for years and for the first time wrote without undue self-consciousness about style or method. "From the first chapter I decided not to 'write' at all," she told Latrobe Carroll in 1921.

And yet there is a similarity between *Alexander's Bridge* and *O Pioneers!* Though the ostensible subject is so different, the tone and feeling worlds apart, and the texture of the prose much more open and even negligent, *O Pioneers!* is handling, in its own way, a theme that is to be found in *Alexander's Bridge,* as it is to be found in Henry James—the relation between the Old World and the New. *Alexander's Bridge* straddles the Atlantic, moving regularly between Boston and London, and an essential part of the novel's atmosphere depends on this juxtaposition of two worlds. In *O Pioneers!* the two worlds are likewise facing each other. Alexandra Bergson, the Swedish heroine, is never wholly freed from her European heritage, and it is the impact of European traditions and sensibilities on the challenging new country that produces the emotional pattern of the novel. The characters are all either immigrants or children of immigrants. Swedish, Czech, German, and French backgrounds intermingle on the Nebraska soil, and the new life that grows up in the American prairie owes its quality and its power, its successes and its failures, to the tension between the Old World and the New.

O Pioneers! is the first of a group of novels in which the impact of a young country on the sad sensitivity of uprooted Europeans is presented with a sympathy and an insight rare in American writers, even the most sophisticated of whom tend to regard the European immigrant as only too happy to leave the bad old world behind and settle down in the land of the free. In *O Pioneers!* as in *The Song of the Lark* and *My Antonia* we find this impact carefully observed, yet in none of these novels is it Miss Cather's main concern. She knows that for the old people, living on their memories of the past, there is no real hope in America, and she symbolizes this in such characters as John Bergson in *O Pioneers!*, Herr Wunsch in *The Song of the Lark,* and Mr. Shimerda in *My Antonia:* she leaves these characters almost abruptly, consigning them without too much compunction to decay and death, and turns to their children to study the much more complex phenomenon of their merging of cultures and backgrounds. On the one hand there is the European heritage, and on the other the open spaces of the American west, with its challenge and excitement and its possibilities of new life for those young and adaptable enough to take them. All these three novels move between these two poles. The most interesting characters

—Alexandra Bergson, Thea Kronborg, Ántonia—owe much of what they are to their European heritage, and it is interesting to note that two of these three at least never give up their parents' language, Ántonia, especially, being found speaking it again at the end of the book, with her young family speaking it around her. Here are no facile studies of children of immigrants being educated or absorbed into "Americanism": Miss Cather knew that Americanism is Europeanism meeting the challenge of a new environment in its own terms.

The strong character is the character who knows what to retain of the past and at the same time how to adapt to the present and the future. That, Miss Cather seems to be saying, is the true pattern of American achievement. The frontier tradition as presented in *O Pioneers!* through the life of Alexandra Bergson becomes significant only when it can fruitfully interact with European memories and ideals, and the same is true of Thea Kronborg in *The Song of the Lark,* though she becomes a famous singer while Alexandra achieves the less spectacular ambition of a prosperous Nebraska farm. In each case we are presented with strength, with character achieving itself. Those characters who never discover in America a challenge to achieve themselves but hanker continually after the old country, remain valuable critical agents, reminders, and warnings against complacent provincialism on either side, and when they are allowed to live (as Carl Linstrum, unlike Mr. Shimerda and similar characters, is allowed) they serve as irritants and gadflies, implicit criticisms, even, of "the American way of life."

Early Novels

It may not be too far-fetched to see in Willa Cather's handling of the European-in-America theme a transmutation of one of James's major themes and thus to recognize James's legacy transplanted and put to new uses. And in other respects the gap between *Alexander's Bridge* and the later novels is not as wide as seems at first sight. The handling of natural description, for example, and the way in which descriptions are placed as prologues or epilogues to episodes depicting character in action, are similar in *Alexander's Bridge* and *O Pioneers!* We have already quoted the descriptive passage which opens *Alexander's Bridge:* we might put beside it the opening of *O Pioneers!:*

One January day, thirty years ago, the little town of Hanover, anchored on a windy Nebraska tableland, was trying not to be blown away. A mist of fine snowflakes was curling and eddying about the cluster of low drab buildings huddled on the gray prairie, under a gray sky. The dwelling-houses were set about haphazard on the tough prairie sod; some of them looked as if they had been moved in overnight, and others as if they were straying off by themselves, headed straight for the open plain. None of them had any appearance of permanence, and the howling wind blew under them as well as over them. The main street was a deeply rutted road, now frozen hard, which ran from the squat red railway station and the grain "elevator" at the north end of the town to the lumber yard and the horse pond at the south end. On either side of this road straggled two uneven rows of wooden buildings; the general merchandise stores, the two banks, the drug store, the feed store, the saloon, the post-office. The board sidewalks were gray with trampled snow, but at two o'clock in the afternoon the shopkeepers, having come back from dinner, were keeping well behind their frosty windows. The children were all in school, and there was nobody abroad in the streets but a few rough-looking countrymen in coarse overcoats, with their long caps pulled down to their noses. Some of them had brought their wives to town, and now and then a red or a plaid shawl flashed out of one store into the shelter of another. At the hitch-bars along the street a few heavy work-horses, harnessed to farm wagons, shivered under their blankets. About the station everything was quiet, for there would not be another train in until night.

There is, of course, difference enough between the two scenes described, but it is the same kind of observation at work. The passage from *O Pioneers!* is the livelier; the details are picked out with a shrewder eye for the effective symbol. (Compare "Some of them had brought their wives to town, and now and then a red or a plaid shawl flashed out of one store into the shelter of another" with: "He crossed Charles Street between jangling street cars and shelving lumber drays.") In spite of the differences, however, we can recognize the *étude* that has developed into a "piece."

The most significant difference between the descriptions in the two novels is that in *Alexander's Bridge* it seems to be merely literary taste that determines what shall be picked out for description or mention ("descending into cooler and cooler depths of grayish shadow;" "the smell of wood smoke in the air, blended with the odor of moist spring earth"), whereas in *O Pioneers!* memory and personal feeling combine with the professional writer's eye and ear to make the selec-

tion. ("The board sidewalks were gray with trampled
snow"— what a different use of "gray" that is from the
"grayish shadow" into which Professor Wilson walked!)
We cannot, however, altogether believe Miss Cather
when she tells us that in *O Pioneers!* she "decided not
to 'write' at all." The opening of the novel is quite carefully wrought, and the quiet close of the paragraph—
"About the station everything was quiet, for there
would not be another train in until night"—is certainly
not the result of automatic writing. It is the result of a
deeply felt emotional pattern manifesting itself not un-
consciously but easily in appropriate images and prose
rhythms.

In an age which has been taught by one of its most
distinguished literary figures that art "is not the expression of personality but an escape from personality"
critics fight shy of recognizing the significance of emotional pattern in a poem or a novel. But whether or not
it is directly related to mere autobiography (and sometimes it is, often it is not), the emotional pattern is one
of the most significant aspects of a fully realized work of
fiction, and discussions of style and structure which ig-
nore this basic element are mere academic exercises. The
emotional pattern might be described as the implicit
sense of value and significance which makes it possible
for a novel to show some things as more worth selecting
and recording than others. It provides the mold in
which the novel is shaped and is, indeed, the original
reason for the novel's being written in the first place.
If we do not recognize it, we can flounder forever among
mere incidents, situations, and descriptions and never

see the novel's underlying rhythm. The trouble with *Alexander's Bridge* is that it has no discernible emotional pattern: the trouble with *O Pioneers!* is that, while it has one, it is consistent neither in strength nor in tenor, and the first part of the novel seems to arise from a different impulse and to be built on different underlying rhythms than those later sections which deal with the love of Emil and Maria and include such unassimilated incidents as the marriage and death of Amédée Chevalier.

Part I of *O Pioneers!*, entitled "The Wild Land," has a strength and individuality that carries the novel along with a splendid vigor. Willa Cather clearly knew where she was going in this section and moves with a fine ease from detailed description to symbolic elaboration and back again:

Although it was only four o'clock, the winter day was fading. The road led southwest, toward the streak of pale, watery light that glimmered in the leaden sky. The light fell upon the two sad young faces that were turned mutely toward it: upon the eyes of the girl, who seemed to be looking with such anguished perplexity into the future; upon the sombre eyes of the boy, who seemed already to be looking into the past. The little town behind them had vanished as if it had never been, had fallen behind the swell of the prairie, and the stern frozen country received them into its bosom. The homesteads were few and far apart; here and there a windmill gaunt against the sky, a sod house crouching in a hollow. But the great fact was the land itself, which seemed to overwhelm the little beginnings of human society that struggled in its sombre wastes. It was from facing this vast hardness that the boy's mouth had become so bitter;

because he felt that men were too weak to make any mark here, that the land wanted to be let alone, to preserve its own fierce strength, its peculiar, savage kind of beauty, its uninterrupted mournfulness.

There is nothing sentimental about such a phrase as "the eyes of the girl, who seemed to be looking with such anguished perplexity into the future," for it arises naturally out of its context and is related to that counterpointing of old and new, past and future, which is one of the main themes of the book and the sole theme of this part of it. Alexander Bergson is driving with her young brother Emil and her friend Carl Linstrum from the little Nebraska town of Hanover home to the farm where her dying father has been for eleven years trying, without any great success, to tame the wild tableland. At this stage all the characters we have so far met are poised between past and future, between memory and desire, between fears and hopes. It remains to be seen whether the hope of eventually taming the land is an illusion or the prelude to heroic achievement. The future lies with those who can harness their imagination to the future without loss of either patience or cunning. John Bergson, who came to the new world to redress the balance of the old, to recover by fresh efforts a fortune lost in Sweden by his father, has made a beginning, but he dies in this opening section of the novel, while the future is still uncertain, and by his death symbolically proclaims that the new world will not respond fully to those who come to it in order to get back what they lost elsewhere, but only to those who see it for what it is and meet it in its own terms. Further, "a pioneer should have imagination, should be able to enjoy the idea of things more than the things themselves." Alexandra, John's determined and far-seeing daughter, can live patiently on confident hopes of the future because she is not trying to get back to where she was but to go forward to where she has never been yet knows she will one day be; she is the appropriate guardian of the wild land until it yields to the efforts of its tamers. There is what might almost be called a mythological element in "The Wild Land," which reappears at intervals throughout the novel.

Part II, "Neighboring Fields," opens sixteen years later. Alexandra, with a combination of prudence and imagination which at the time often puzzled and annoyed her less interesting and more conventionally minded younger brothers, Oscar and Lou, had refused to part with any of their land even in the most difficult years and had instead regularly acquired the land of those who gave up and returned to an urban life. Her instinct proved right; and in this section of the book we see her the prosperous owner of much wealthy farm land. For the wild land has at last blossomed, and John Bergson would not recognize it if he could rise from the grave:

The shaggy coat of the prairie, which they lifted to make him a bed, has vanished forever. From the Norwegian graveyard one looks out over a vast checker-board, marked off in squares of wheat and corn; light and dark, dark and light. Telephone wires hum along the white roads, which always run at right angles. From the graveyard gate one can count a dozen gayly painted farmhouses; the gilded weather-vanes on the big red barns wink at each other across the green and brown and yellow fields.

The future has triumphed, and a new, almost lyrical note emerges in the rhythms of the prose:

There are few scenes more gratifying than a spring plowing in that country, where the furrows of a single field often lie a mile in length, and the brown earth, with such a strong, clean smell, and such a power of growth and fertility in it, yields itself eagerly to the plow; rolls away from the shear, not even dimming the brightness of the metal, with a soft, deep sigh of happiness. The wheat-cutting sometimes goes on all night as well as all day, and in good seasons there are scarcely men and horses enough to do the harvesting. The grain is so heavy that it bends toward the blade and cuts like velvet.

This new note, occurring when only a quarter of the book has been completed, makes it clear that the main theme of the novel is not to be the conquering of the wild land by the pioneers, helped and hindered by hopes and memories. Miss Cather has to move the story into a new key in order to keep it going. It is true that in the character of Alexandra's sensitive younger brother Emil and the brief but significant introduction of the attractive "little Bohemian girl" Marie Tovesky she had in Part I laid the foundations for new developments; but nothing in the opening section really prepares us for the road the book is now to take. Emil falls in love with the sprightly Marie, now married to a surly and suspicious husband. Carl Linstrum, Alexandra's childhood friend, returns from the city on a visit, and their contemplated marriage is for the time being at least frustrated by suspicion, timidity of mind, and an ungenerous attitude on the part of Oscar and Lou. As these events unfold, the European backgrounds are developed and displayed: the Bohemian background of Marie and her family, the French background of Amédée, and the ever-present Swedish atmosphere of Alexandra and her neighbors. We get a sense of the Old World being absorbed in the New, though always with some elements remaining intractable, like eccentric old Ivar or the nostalgic Mrs. Lee, who is kept from her old-world habits by a daughter and son-in-law who are eager to keep up with the Joneses and follow what they deem to be the latest city fashions. (This is an example of the assimilated generation being narrower and less admirable people than their immigrant parents.) There is an almost episodic quality about this phase of *O Pioneers!* But by the time the section has come to an end we are aware of the dangerous potentialities of the relation between Emil and Marie and of Alexandra's discouragement when she has to let her lover go because he is not strong enough to face down public opinion.

Part III, a brief section of less than twenty pages entitled "Winter Memories," presents an atmosphere of waiting and mounting tension against a background of frozen winter exteriors and warm domestic interiors. Again the opening is a set piece of description:

Winter has settled down over the Divide again; the season in which Nature recuperates, in which she sinks to sleep between the fruitfulness of autumn and the passion of spring. The birds have gone. The teeming life that goes on down in the long grass is exterminated. The prairie-dog keeps his hole. The rabbits run shivering from one frozen garden patch to another and are hard put to it to find frost-bitten cabbage-stalks. At night the coyotes roam the wintry waste, howling for food. The variegated fields are all one color now; the pastures, the stubble, the roads, the sky are the same leaden gray. The hedgerows and trees are scarcely perceptible against the bare earth, whose slaty hue they have taken on. The ground is frozen so hard that it bruises the foot to walk in the roads or in the ploughed fields. It is like an iron country, and the spirit is oppressed by its rigor and melancholy. One could easily believe that in that dead landscape the germs of life and fruitfulness were extinct forever.

It is in passages such as these that the emotional pattern of the novel is most clearly visible. The human drama is subordinated to the drama of the plains and the seasons, and the characters seem less interesting than the background against which they move.

The tragedy emerges in Part IV, "The White Mulberry Tree," where Emil, returned from Mexico, is discovered with Marie by Marie's wild and sulky husband, who shoots and kills them both. Shortly before this the gay and confident Amédée, now the father of a recently born son, dies suddenly of appendicitis. The violent double intrusion of death into the picture of a new social life flowering under the impact of an old people on a new land shatters the surface of the novel somewhat; but the shattering is deliberate and evidently meant to suggest that once life has put down roots anything may happen. The final section brings Alexandra and Carl together again, and the book ends by reestablishing an earlier note: "Fortunate country, that is one day to receive hearts like Alexandra's into its bosom, to give them out again in the yellow wheat, in the rustling corn, in the shining eyes of youth!" This is less a resolution of the personal tragedy which the novel unfolds, than an ignoring of it. We are back to the pioneering theme again, to the lyrical mood of reminiscence and wonder. The novel has no real "katharsis," because it ends by turning away from the tragic elements rather than by subsuming them in a larger pattern. Yet, since the fate of the other characters has really been incidental to the real theme of the novel, this ending is not altogether inappropriate. It establishes Alexandra as a kind of Earth Mother or Corn Goddess, a Ceres who presides over the fruitful land, symbol of the success of the pioneers in taming the reluctant but immensely promising soil. Beside her the love of Emil and Marie and their death together seem like a feverish episode outside the main stream of events.

Alexandra is not a character whom we are allowed to know intimately or who is even convincing as a creation. She moves with a calm, symbolic motion throughout the book against a background of golden corn and agricultural routine. The acting out of a more intimately human drama is left to the minor characters, who, if of lesser stature, are more idiosyncratic and lively. Willa Cather was combining her own deep-seated feeling about the country of the pioneers, with its almost mythological suggestions of growth, fertility, and rural richness, with memories of particular people and events. "*O Pioneers!* interested me tremendously," she wrote later, "because it had to do with a kind of country I loved, because it was about old neighbors, once very dear, whom I had almost forgotten in the hurry and excitement of growing up and finding out what the world was like and trying to get on in it." [2] This interest gives the novel much of its strength and vitality—it is one of the strongest of Willa Cather's novels—though it may account at the same time for disparate elements in it which are never wholly resolved into a unity. Episodic and unevenly patterned as it is, *O Pioneers!* has nevertheless moments of strange force and beauty and a general air of power and assurance which are remarkable enough and proclaim a significant talent.

There are equal power and even greater richness in *The Song of the Lark* (1915), the story of how the daughter of a Swedish Methodist pastor in Moonstone, Colorado, became a great opera singer. This is a remarkable novel in many ways: the fierce concentration on the processes by which an artist finds herself; the vigorous and vivid presentation of scene after scene and incident after incident which illustrate the development of the heroine's potentialities under the impact both of circumstances and the drive of her own character; the sympathy and insight with which Miss Cather shows "how the people in little desert towns live by the railway and order their lives by the coming and going of the trains" and her whole sense of the significance of railroading to the West; the preoccupation with musical achievement and musical standards, which sets the

[2] "My First Novels."

whole story against a background of musical endeavor; the shrewd understanding of the conflict between those characters whose perception and ambitions are limited by the conventions of provincial complacency and those who instinctively feel the need to escape from such limitations (a common conflict in Miss Cather's early novels: it is a variation of the conflict between Alexandra Bergson and her two brothers in *O Pioneers!*); the feeling for places with their special colors and flavors derived partly from geography and partly from history—these are only some of the elements crowded into this novel which, for all the singleness of its theme, is nevertheless richer in texture than anything its author had yet written.

Looking back on the novel some sixteen years later, Willa Cather was inclined to agree with earlier critics who thought, as Heinemann, the London publisher, expressed it, that "the full-blooded method, which told everything about everybody, was not natural to [her] and was not the one in which [she] would ever take satisfaction." [3] Though she did not accept this judgment at the time, she wrote in 1931 that "too much detail is apt, like any other form of extravagance, to become slightly vulgar; and it quite destroys in a book a very satisfying element analogous to what painters call 'composition.'" [4] Though it is the abundance of detail that gives the book its peculiar strength and richness, the element of "composition" in the novel is not altogether satisfactory, and in order to shake the book down into

[3] *Ibid.*
[4] *Ibid.*

some order and pattern a number of shoddy devices had to be used. Fred Ottenburg, for example, sympathetic, handsome, and musical beer king, steps in as *deus ex machina* to rescue the heroine from depression and exhaustion following a spell of work with an able but unsympathetic singing teacher in Chicago, sets her up, and renews her ambition by giving her a wonderful holiday in a ranch in Arizona by "a whole cañon full of Cliff-Dweller ruins." However, since it would spoil this record of an artist's progress to have her marry at this stage in her career, Miss Cather invents a thoroughly unconvincing situation—Fred is already married to a hysterical and eventually deranged wife, from whom he is separated; Thea Kronborg, the heroine, agrees to marry him without knowing this, and when the news is finally broken she is shocked and angered and goes off to Germany to study alone. Fred must be around to help, but he cannot be allowed to clutter up Thea's emotional life, so he is manipulated around her with a delicately artificial pirouetting which is on a completely different level of probability from the main story.

The first part of the novel is set in Moonstone. We first see Thea as an eleven-year-old girl being brought out of a serious case of pneumonia by Dr. Howard Archie. Dr. Archie is handsome, imaginative, unhappily married, not altogether adjusted to the limitations of Moonstone life, and from the beginning deeply interested in and attracted by Thea. He, too, is a *deus ex machina*—it is he who lends Thea the money to enable her to study in Germany; and there is yet another *deus* in the person of Ray Kennedy, freight train conductor on the run between Moonstone and Denver, who adores Thea and plans to marry her when she is old enough. When Ray is killed in a railroad accident it is discovered that his life was insured for six hundred dollars in Thea's favor to enable her to take music lessons in Chicago.

Both Dr. Archie and Fred Ottenburg are conventional romantic characters who exist in order to help the heroine along. Ray Kennedy, however, is drawn with much more conviction. He represents the best that Thea could have hoped for if she had been content with the limitations of the Moonstone world, and the fact that he serves only to provide her with a means of escape from that world is symbolic of Thea's relations with her early environment. Willa Cather was perfectly aware of the way in which she used these three men to facilitate her heroine's escape, and in a preface to the novel written in 1932 she wrote: "What I cared about, and still care about, was the girl's escape; the play of blind chance, the way in which commonplace occurrences fell together to liberate her from commonness. She seemed wholly at the mercy of accident; but to persons of her vitality and honesty, fortunate accidents will always happen." This is a legitimate defense of the use of *dei ex machina* in a novel of this kind; but this does not absolve the novelist from the responsibility of making the characters who play this liberating part operate on the same level of probability as the main action.

The first section of the novel, "Friends of Childhood," is a complete and satisfying story in itself. It is the story of Thea Kronborg's life from the age of eleven until, just seventeen, she sets out for Chicago for a winter of music study on Ray Kennedy's six hundred dollars. Every aspect of the impact of her environment on Thea which can bring out her difference from the ordinary citizens of Moonstone and develop her own awareness of her gift is presented in a mood of almost passionate exploration. She takes piano lessons from Herr Wunsch, a broken-down German. Once a distinguished musician but now a drunken failure, Wunsch has drifted from one town to another, conscious of his own progressive disintegration and haunted by memories, until he is rescued and temporarily rehabilitated by Fritz Kohler, the town tailor, and his wife, fellow Germans with an affectionate interest in him. During the few years that he survives in Moonstone, before leaving the town after breaking out in a drunken frenzy, he has managed to teach Thea all he knows and to discover something of her immense promise. Thea's relation with Wunsch and the Kohlers takes her out of Moonstone into an old-world atmosphere full of old-world dreams and memories. The language spoken in the Kohler house is German, and Thea picks up enough of it to sing German songs and follow a German conversation.

The German artist-professor is something of a stock figure in American fiction, but the broken-down Wunsch is a strongly drawn character in his own right who is saved from sentimentality by his obvious imperfections. Embittered by years of teaching provincial American misses with no musical intelligence and no musical ambition other than to play something showy in a pretty dress at a church concert, frustrated by life in a new and raw part of the country which knows nothing of the mellow traditions of art and has no conception of the fierce demands made by standards of artistic integrity, Wunsch finds at last in Thea someone to whom he can express something of all this, even though she, an excited and bewildered girl in her early teens, does not altogether understand what he is talking about. His outbursts confirm her own as yet only half-understood artistic instinct. She has always known that she was different; and slowly she discovers how and why.

The Old World reaches out to Moonstone and makes contact with Thea Kronborg's hopes and ambitions. This is yet another aspect of that continuous interest in the impact of the Old World on the New that is such a dominant theme in Willa Cather's fiction. For all her passionate interest in the American West and her lively and sympathetic descriptions of the sights and sounds of those parts of it which she knew—and the first half of this novel is full of such descriptions—it is always the touch from the Old World that fulfills the potentialities of American character. The mellowness, the leisureliness, the distrust of mere material progress that the older immigrant brings are always seen by Miss Cather as necessary for a proper fertilization of the American cultural soil. If these qualities do not come from Europe, they must come from south of the Border.

The old folk, the immigrants who never fully adjust to the new American life, are here as elsewhere in Willa Cather's novels often contrasted favorably with their better adjusted children. The young Kohlers "were ashamed of their old folks and got out into the world as fast as possible; had their clothes made by a Denver tailor and their necks shaved up under their hair and forgot the past." Old Fritz Kohler and his lodger Herr Wunsch never forgot the past: it haunted them and prevented them from finding full satisfaction in America:

The two men were like comrades; perhaps the bond between them was the glass wherein lost hopes are found; perhaps it was common memories of another country; perhaps it was the grape-vine in the garden—the knotty, fibrous shrub, full of homesickness and sentiment, which the Germans have carried around the world with them.

Thea found herself responding to this Old World atmosphere, as she found herself responding to the bright and colorful life of the Mexicans, who lived in the unfashionable part of Moonstone east of Main Street. Her relations with the Mexicans, and particularly with the picturesque and volatile Spanish Johnny, who has the habit of wandering off unpredictably for months on end to make his living as an itinerant minstrel south of the Border and then reappearing in a state of utter exhaustion, are part of her self-discovery as an artist. This aspect of the story is worked out with care and skill, and provides some memorable scenes, in particular the description of a dance in Mexican Town, followed by an informal concert at which Thea sings. The contrast between the uninhibited love of music which Thea finds in Mexican Town and the stuffy conventions and petty jealousies which surround the annual Sunday School Concert given by the "respectable" element in Moonstone forms part of the pattern of the whole first section of the novel.

Once Thea has left Moonstone the novel loses much of its interest. The story of her stay in Chicago is told in convincing detail, with a fine sense of what was going on in Chicago musical circles during the early years of Theodore Thomas' leadership (there is a note of real comedy here), but the interest becomes more and more purely documentary, and the temperature of the novel falls rapidly. In her 1932 preface Miss Cather wrote: "The chief fault of the book is that it describes a descending curve; the life of a successful artist in the full tide of achievement is not so interesting as the life of a talented young girl 'fighting her way,' as we say. Success is never so interesting as struggle—not even to the successful, not even to the most mercenary forms of ambition." This is true enough, but it does not quite explain why the crucial years of Thea's struggle, when she is alone and fighting her way in an indifferent world, are less interesting than the story of her early life, before she had fully realized her own talent and ambition. It seems that Mr. Heinemann was right: she had simply put too much into the novel.

Writing on the art of fiction in 1920, Willa Cather remarked:

Art, it seems to me, should simplify. That, indeed, is very nearly the whole of the higher artistic process; finding what conventions of form and what detail one can do without and yet preserve the spirit of the whole—so that all that one has suppressed and cut away is there to the reader's consciousness as much as if it were in type on the page.

She may have been thinking of *The Song of the Lark* and its shortcomings when she wrote this. Certainly, she never returned to this "full-blooded method" in her subsequent novels.

But this method has its compensations. There is scene after scene in the Chicago section of the book which has a strength and urgency of presentation that arrest and excite the reader. The careful investigation of Thea's relation to her piano teacher Harsanyi; the impressive scene at the Harsanyis where she first reveals the immense promise of her voice; the alternation of excitement, dogged determination, sheer exhaustion, and unformulated ambitions which we are shown as the accompaniment of Thea's progress as a student; the contrast between Thea in moments of a musical exaltation and Thea in an unsympathetic and inhibiting environment; the illuminating study of how musical intelligence shows itself both in musical achievement and in daily activity—there is material in all this for a dozen novels. And perhaps that it what is wrong: too much of it is material for novels and not enough is fully integrated into the pattern of the work as a whole. One must not labor this point; there is no doubt that *The Song of the Lark* is in its way a remarkable novel; yet, impressive though it is, it is not wholly satisfactory.

The interlude in Arizona among the Cliff-Dweller ruins, in spite of the thinness of the motivation which leads up to it, is in itself remarkably well done and possesses a lyrical quality of the kind which emerges occasionally in *O Pioneers!*—a quality which Willa Cather kept in reserve to release when she felt the pattern of the novel most needed it. The reader needs it here as much as Thea needed her Arizona vacation.

This Arizona vacation marks an important crisis in Thea's life: she finally puts her past behind her and decides to go to Germany to study. Wandering and meditating among the ruins of an ancient Indian civilization she gets a new perspective on her own life:

It was while she was in this abstracted state, waiting for the clock to strike, that Thea at last made up her mind what she was going to try to do in the world, and that she was going to Germany to study without further loss of time. Only by the merest chance had she ever got to Panther Cañon. There was certainly no kindly Providence that directed one's life; and one's parents did not in the least care what became of one, so long as one did not misbehave and endanger their comfort. One's life was at the mercy of blind chance. She had better take it in her own hands and lose everything than meekly draw the plough under the rod of parental guidance. She had seen it when she was at home last summer—the hostility of comfortable, self-satisfied people toward any serious effort. Even to her father it seemed indecorous. Whenever she spoke seriously, he looked apologetic. Yet she had clung fast to whatever was left of Moonstone in her mind. No more of that! The Cliff-Dwellers had lengthened her past. She had older and higher obligations.

In her best work, Willa Cather always surrounds her moments of crisis with an appropriate mood derived from natural description. We have seen how she did this in *O Pioneers!*, and here again the note of lyrical description emerges at this critical moment:

At last a kind of hopefulness broke in the air. In a moment the pine trees up on the edge of the rim were flashing with coppery fire. The thin red clouds which hung above their pointed tops began to boil and move rapidly, weaving in and out like smoke. The swallows darted out of their rock-houses as at a signal, and flew upward, toward the rim. Little brown birds began to chirp in the bushes along the watercourse down at the bottom of the ravine, where everything was still dusky and pale. At first the golden light seemed to hang like a wave upon the rim of the cañon; the trees and bushes up there, which one scarcely noticed at noon, stood out magnified by the slanting rays. Long, thin streaks of light began to reach quiveringly down into the gorge. The red sun rose rapidly above the tops of the blazing pines, and its glow burst into the gulf, about the very doorstep on which Thea sat. It bored into the wet, dark underbrush. The dripping cherry bushes, the pale aspens, and the frosty *piñons* were glittering and trembling, swimming in the liquid gold. All the pale, dusty little herbs of the bean family, never seen by anyone but a botanist, became for a moment individual and important, their silky leaves quite beautiful with dew and light. The arch of sky overhead, heavy as lead a little while before, lifted, became more and more transparent, and one could look up into depths of pearly blue.

In the final section of the book we see Thea in the full tide of her success. She has returned from Germany to sing Wagner at the Metropolitan Opera House in New York. The sudden collapse of the principal soprano after the first act gives her the chance to take over the part of Sieglinde in *Die Walküre,* and her resounding success in this part, in spite of having to take it on at a moment's notice, assures her position. The interest of the novel now lies in the effect of this continuous endeavor on Thea's character and on her relations with Dr. Archie and Fred Ottenburg (she is now perfectly reconciled with Fred, who is awaiting the death of his estranged and mentally diseased wife before marrying her). There are some carefully presented scenes here, with the artist's moments of exaltation and exhaustion convincingly portrayed; but by this time the reader is inclined to feel that the whole business has been rather too long drawn out. The novel ends with a return to Moonstone, where we see Thea's Aunt Tillie, the last survivor of her family left in the town, basking in the reflected glory of her niece's success. The book is rounded out with a paragraph which seeks to explore the meaning of the relation between those who go out into the world and make a name for themselves and the routine lives of those who stay at home:

However much they may smile at her, the old inhabitants would miss Tillie. Her stories give them something to talk about and to conjecture about, cut off as they are from the restless currents of the world. The many naked little sandbars which lie between Venice and the mainland, in the seemingly stagnant water of the lagoons, are made habitable and wholesome only because, every night, a foot and a half of tide creeps in from the sea and winds its fresh brine up through all that network of shining waterways. So, into all the little settlements of quiet people, tidings of what their boys and girls are doing in the world bring refreshment; bring to the old, memories, and to the young, dreams.

This ending, written with a deliberate sententiousness which is not ineffective, seems, nevertheless, to have little relation to the main theme of the novel. The story thus seems to end on an afterthought.

The Song of the Lark is full of impressive insights into the life of the musical artist and shows a wealth of musical intelligence adroitly put at the service of character study. Willa Cather had learned from Gertrude Hall's *The Wagnerian Romances*—a book which, with Bernard Shaw's *The Perfect Wagnerite,* she regarded as constituting the "only two books in English on the Wagnerian operas that are at all worthy of their subject"—to "reproduce the emotional effect of one art through the medium of another art." In spite of its faults of structure and proportion it is impossible not to recognize that this novel is the work of a strong and original talent.

Willa Cather revised the novel in 1937. The changes she made were not extensive, consisting mainly of a judicious pruning of some of the more detailed and less relevant descriptions. The description of Tillie's activities in the Epilogue is abbreviated, to good effect. A good example of the tightening achieved by the revision can be found in the conclusion of the penultimate paragraph. In the original version it reads:

. . . A boy grew up on one of those streets who went to Omaha and built up a great business, and is now very rich. Moonstone people always speak of him and Thea together, as examples of Moonstone enterprise. They do, however, talk oftener of Thea. A voice has even a wider appeal than a fortune. It is the gift that all creatures would possess if they could. Dreary Maggie Evans dead nearly twenty years, is still remembered because Thea sang at her funeral "after she had studied in Chicago."

In the revised version the paragraph ends with the sentence "A voice has even wider appeal than a fortune," the following two sentences being omitted. The gain is obvious. Some of the changes are very slight but are interesting in that they suggest that the book was originally written fairly fast, without too much attention to the workmanship of the individual sentence, which is sometimes improved in the revision by the omission or addition of a single word. For example, while the original text has: "On Friday afternoon there was an inspiring audience; there was not an empty chair in the house," the revision has: "On Friday afternoon there was an inspiring audience; not an empty chair in the house." This is a trivial enough change; but it indicates either an improvement in Miss Cather's ear for prose rhythms, or else a certain haste and carelessness in the original writing.

CHAPTER 3

Decline of the West

My Antonia, which appeared in 1918, is another story of pioneering life in Nebraska. Like *O Pioneers!* it contains autobiographical elements—the heroine was suggested by "a Bohemian girl who was good to me when I was a child"—and is concerned with the conflict between memory and desire, nostalgia and ambition, in the immigrant. The European background, which lies behind the book like a fascinating mystery, is both attractive and disturbing: the picturesque and feudal Bohemia for which Mr. Shimerda languishes is but one aspect of a background which includes the horror of the Russian scene where famished wolves pursue a bridal party returning home during the night. Yet, for all the tensions between the Old World and the New to be found in this novel as in so many of the others, the central theme is neither the struggle of the pioneer nor the conflict between generations, but the development and self-discovery of the heroine. This suggests a structure like that of *The Song of the Lark;* but in fact the book is organized much more like *O Pioneers!* We do not follow the heroine's career in the anxious detail we find in the

43

preceding novel. Although Willa Cather did not at the time agree with Mr. Heinemann's criticism of *The Song of the Lark* and its "full-blooded method," she tells us that "when the next book, *My Antonia,* came along, quite of itself and with no direction from me, it took the road of *O Pioneers!*—not the road of *The Song of the Lark.*"

The story is told in the first person by Jim Burden, childhood friend of the heroine and now "legal counsel for one of the great Western railways." This device gives proper voice to the autobiographical impulse which lies behind much of the book; but it has its dangers. No observer, however knowing and sympathetic, can tell the full story of the development of a character like Ántonia. A character who is constantly talked about, described, and discussed but who never reveals herself fully and directly to the reader tends to become the kind of symbol the observer wants to make of her, an objectification of the observer's emotions, and this in large measure does happen to Ántonia. Her growth, development, and final adjustment is a vast symbolic progress interesting less for what it is than for what it can be made to mean.

This is in some degree true also of Alexandra Bergson in *O Pioneers!,* who emerges at the end of the book as a kind of Earth Goddess symbolic of what the pioneers had achieved on the Nebraska plains. There is an epic quality in *O Pioneers!* which makes one resent the intrusion of incidents drawn to a smaller scale. That epic quality is lacking in *My Antonia:* the cultivation of the land is not something *achieved* by Antonia, but something in which she submerges herself in order to attain salvation. She ends as the ideal wife and mother, bound to the farming life, more devoted than ever to the open spaces: but it is not she who has made that life possible or tamed those open spaces so much as it is that life and those spaces which have saved her.

Throughout the book the narrator's sensibility takes control; and this raises problems which Willa Cather is never quite able to solve. The narrator's development goes on side by side with Ántonia's: indeed, we sometimes lose sight of Ántonia for long stretches at a time, while we can never lose sight of the narrator. Miss Cather tries to solve this problem by emphasizing that the book's title is *My Ántonia:* this is not just the story of Ántonia, but of Ántonia as she impinged on a number of other significant characters. She goes out of the way to use the adjective "my" in talking of Ántonia with reference not only to the narrator but also to other characters—to her father, who first uses the phrase, and to Mrs. Steavens, for example. And yet we cannot say that this is a story of what Ántonia meant to a selected number of other characters of the book: though there are elements in the story which suggest this, the organization as a whole tends to present Ántonia as a symbolic figure in her own right rather than as a character with special meaning for particular individuals.

Some of these points may be made clearer by a more detailed discussion of the story. It opens with the arrival of Jim Burden, the narrator, at his grandparents' farm in Nebraska: he has been sent there from Virginia at the age of ten on the death of his parents (Willa Cather, too, had come from Virginia to Nebraska as a child).

The Shimerdas arrive from Bohemia at the same time to settle in a raw neighboring farm whose ill-kept sod house provides a sad contrast to the fine wooden house of Jim's grandparents. The Shimerdas were the first Bohemian family to come to that part of the country. "They could not speak enough English to ask for advice, or even to make their most pressing wants known." Mr. Shimerda, cultured, melancholy, completely lost in this rough new country, lives in the past, having lost the will to adjust, and ends by committing suicide. His wife, an altogether less refined and coarser person, complains and bullies her way along until, with the assistance of neighbors, her situation improves. His nineteen-year-old son Ambrosch, to advance whose fortunes Mrs. Shimerda had insisted on emigrating to America, is sullen, insensitive, hard-working, and cunning. There is another son, who is mentally deficient and plays but a small part in the story. Then there is Ántonia, four years older than Jim, with brown hair, brown skin, golden-brown eyes, and a personality rich enough to make up for all deficiencies in other members of her family. Ántonia has a younger sister, Yulka, whose role is quite minor.

The relation between the Burdens and the Shimerdas is at the beginning that of relatively prosperous neighbors to a distressed immigrant family. The Shimerdas had not been fairly dealt with by the Bohemian homesteader from whom they had bought their land and sod house, and they found conditions appalling on arrival. Had it not been for the assistance of the Burdens they would not have survived their first winter in Nebraska.

Jim and Ántonia are thrown together from the beginning, and from the beginning Antonia, in spite of her fragmentary English and humbler circumstances, is the dominating character. Together they explore the countryside and learn to know and love the Nebraska plains. Incidents are contrived by the author to bring out different aspects of the Nebraska scene and atmosphere, and there is some impressive descriptive writing.

There are episodes in this first part of the book that have little if any relation to the story of Ántonia's development—the story of the two Russians, Peter and Pavel, for example. Mr. Shimerda, who could understand their language, made friends with them, but soon afterward Pavel died, and on his deathbed he told the terrible story of how as a young man in Russia he had thrown a bride and groom off a sledge to the pursuing wolves in order to save himself from certain death. This is a remarkable little inset story, but its relation to the novel as a whole is somewhat uncertain. It was soon after the death of Pavel and the subsequent departure of Peter that Mr. Shimerda committed suicide. By this time it was midwinter, and the atmosphere of the frozen landscape is effectively employed to emphasize the pity and horror of this death from homesickness.

Mr. Shimerda had hoped to see Ántonia get a good American education, but after his death she took her place as one of the workers on the farm, to which she devoted all her time.

When the sun was dropping low, Ántonia came up the big south draw with her team. How much older she had grown in eight months! She had come to us a child, and now she was a tall, strong young girl, although her fifteenth birthday had just slipped by. I ran out and met her as she brought her horses up to the windmill to water them. She wore the boots her father had so thoughtfully taken off before he shot himself, and his old fur cap. Her outgrown cotton dress switched about her calves, over the boot-tops. She kept her sleeves rolled up all day, and her arms and throat were burned as brown as a sailor's. Her neck came up strongly out of her shoulders, like the bole of a tree out of the turf. One sees that draught-horse neck among the peasant women in all old countries.

For all her devotion to her father's memory, Mr. Shimerda's mantle does not fall on Antonia, but rather on Jim, who responds to the suggestion of a rich European culture lying behind his melancholy. This is the first of a series of influences that lead him eventually to the university and a professional career in the East, yet in a profound if indirect way it draws him closer to Ántonia.

Jim goes to school while Ántonia works on the farm:

"I came to ask you something, Tony. Grandmother wants to know if you can't go to the term of school that begins next week over at the sod school-house. She says there's a good teacher, and you'd learn a lot."

Ántonia stood up, lifting and dropping her shoulders as if they were stiff. "I ain't got time to learn. I can work like mans now. My mother can't say no more how Ambrosch do all and nobody to help him. I can work as much as him. School is all right for little boys. I help make this land one good farm."

She clucked to her team and started for the barn. I walked beside her, feeling vexed. Was she going to grow up boastful like her mother, I wondered? Before we reached the stable,

Decline of the West

I felt something tense in her silence, and glancing up I saw that she was crying. She turned her face from me and looked off at the red streak of dying light, over the dark prairie.

I climbed up into the loft and threw down the hay for her, while she unharnessed her team. We walked slowly back toward the house. Ambrosch had come in from the north quarter, and was watering his oxen at the tank.

Ántonia took my hand. "Sometime you will tell me all those nice things you learn at the school, won't you, Jimmy?" she asked with a sudden rush of feeling in her voice. "My father, he went much to school. He know a great deal; how to make the fine cloth like what you not got here. He play horn and violin, and he read so many books that the priests in Bohemie come to talk to him. You won't forget my father, Jim?"

"No," I said, "I will never forget him."

The first section of *My Ántonia* ends with a brilliant summer scene. Ántonia and Jim watch an electric storm from the slanting roof of the Burdens' chicken house:

The thunder was loud and metallic, like the rattle of sheet iron, and the lightning broke in great zigzags across the heavens, making everything stand out and come close to us for a moment. Half the sky was chequered with black thunderheads, but all the west was luminous and clear: in the lightning flashes it looked like deep blue water, with the sheen of moonlight on it; and the mottled part of the sky was like marble pavement, like the quay of some splendid sea-coast city, doomed to destruction. Great warm splashes of rain fell on our upturned faces. One black cloud, no bigger than a little boat, drifted out into the clear space unattended, and kept moving westward. All about us we could hear the felty beat of the raindrops on the soft dust of the farmyard.

Grandmother came to the door and said it was late, and we would get wet out there.

"In a minute we come," Antonia called back to her. "I like your grandmother, and all things here," she sighed. "I wish my papa live to see this summer. I wish no winter ever come again."

"It will be summer a long while yet," I reassured her. "Why aren't you always nice like this, Tony?"

"How nice?"

"Why, just like this; like yourself. Why do you all the time try to be like Ambrosch?"

She put her arms under her head and lay back, looking up at the sky. "If I live here, like you, that is different. Things will be easy for you. But they will be hard for us."

After three years on the farm Jim and his grandparents move to the "clean, well-planted little prairie town" of Black Hawk. The second section of the book concerns life in Black Hawk. Antonia has to be brought in, so Miss Cather contrives to have her engaged as a cook by the Harlings, the family who live next door to the Burdens in their new home. It is, perhaps, a rather artificial device to move the heroine temporarily into the narrator's town in order to keep her under his eye, but the sequence of events which brings this about are not improbable in terms of the story as told. What is more dubious is the relation of this whole section of the novel to the main theme of the story. It is in itself a brilliantly written section. Life in the small prairie town is described with a cunning eye for the significant detail, and a fine emotional rhythm runs through the whole. The daughters of the immigrant (mostly Swedish) farmers

in the country round about have come into town to get
positions as maids and thereby help their families to
improve their economic position: Jim and Tony move
happily in these humble circles, whose healthy gaiety is
sharply contrasted with the narrow stuffiness of the
tradespeople and their families.

Those girls had grown up in the first bitter-hard times,
and had got little schooling themselves. But the younger
brothers and sisters, for whom they made such sacrifices
and who have had "advantages," never seem to me, when
I meet them now, half as interesting or as well educated.
The older girls, who helped to break up the wild sod,
learned so much from life, from poverty, from their mothers
and grandmothers; they had all, like Ántonia, been early
awakened and made observant by coming at a tender age
from an old country to a new.

I can remember a score of these country girls who were in
service in Black Hawk during the few years I lived there,
and I can remember something unusual and engaging
about each of them. Physically they were almost a race apart,
and out-of-door work had given them a vigour which, when
they got over their first shyness on coming to town, developed into a positive carriage and freedom of movement,
and made them conspicuous among Black Hawk women.

The feeling that it is the imaginative immigrant and
not the stuffy conventional American who is responsible
for the country's greatness recurs again and again in
Miss Cather's novels:

The daughters of Black Hawk merchants had a confident,
unenquiring belief that they were "refined," and that the
country girls, who "worked out," were not. The American

farmers in our country were quite as hard-pressed as their neighbours from other countries. All alike had come to Nebraska with little capital and no knowledge of the soil they must subdue. All had borrowed money on their land. But no matter in what straits the Pennsylvanian or Virginian found himself, he would not let his daughters go out into service. Unless his girls could teach a country school, they sat at home in poverty.

The Bohemian and Scandinavian girls could not get positions as teachers, because they had no opportunity to learn the language. Determined to help in the struggle to clear the homestead from debt, they had no alternative but to go into service. . . . But every one of them did what she had set out to do, and sent home those hard-earned dollars. The girls I knew were always helping to pay for ploughs and reapers, brood-sows, or steers to fatten.

One result of this family solidarity was that the foreign farmers in our country were the first to become prosperous. After the fathers were out of debt, the daughters married the sons of neighbours—usually of like nationality—and the girls who once worked in Black Hawk kitchens are to-day managing big farms and fine families of their own; their children are better off than the children of the town women they used to serve.

I thought the attitude of the town people toward these girls very stupid. If I told my schoolmates that Lena Lingard's grandfather was a clergyman, and much respected in Norway, they looked at me blankly. What did it matter? All foreigners were ignorant people who couldn't speak English. There was not a man in Black Hawk who had the intelligence or cultivation, much less the personal distinction, of Antonia's father. Yet people saw no difference be-

tween her and the three Marys; they were all Bohemians, all
"hired girls."

I always knew I should live long enough to see my country
girls come into their own, and I have. . . .

A passage such as this is not the sociological digression
it might at first sight seem: it helps to set the emotional
tone of this section of the novel and is not unrelated to
the main theme of Antonia's development. Yet there is
much in the description of life in Black Hawk which
is not part of this pattern, but of the quite different
pattern of the development and career of Jim Burden.
These final years at high school before moving on to the
University of Nebraska were of course very significant
in Jim's career, as they were in that of Miss Cather, who
followed a similar progress. Antonia plays a very minor
part in this section, while the gradually maturing Jim
looks out in excitement and growing understanding on
the social scene in Black Hawk. Is it that Jim is fitting
himself to be the ideal observer of Ántonia? That seems
to be the only way in which this part of the novel can
be structurally justified.

But, as we have noted, the section considered by itself is a remarkable piece of writing. The account of
the Harling family, the extraordinary story of Mr. and
Mrs. Cutter, scenes at the Boys' Home ("the best hotel
on our branch of the Burlington"), the Saturday night
dances in the tent set up on the vacant lot, the blind
Negro pianist playing at the hotel, and through it all
the good-humored and purposeful "hired girls" moving
with a freedom and vitality that put the middle-class

females of Black Hawk to shame—in this kind of descriptive writing Miss Cather was doing for her part of the country something of what Sarah Orne Jewett had done for New England. There is the flavor of a region and of a community here, and we can see why, in turning to this phase of her story, Willa Cather occasionally lost sight of her main theme.

A scene such as this, in the hotel, has real flavor to it:

When I stole into the parlour, Anson Kirkpatrick, Marshall Field's man, was at the piano, playing airs from a musical comedy then running in Chicago. He was a dapper little Irishman, very vain, homely as a monkey, with friends everywhere, and a sweetheart in every port, like a sailor. I did not know all the men who were sitting about, but I recognized a furniture salesman from Kansas City, a drug man, and Willy O'Reilly, who travelled for a jewellery house and sold musical instruments. The talk was all about good and bad hotels, actors and actresses and musical prodigies. I learned that Mrs. Gardener had gone to Omaha to hear Booth and Barrett, who were to play there next week, and that Mary Anderson was having a great success in "A Winter's Tale," in London.

Or consider this winter scene, which can be set beside the opening scene in *O Pioneers!*:

If I loitered on the playground after school, or went to the post-office for the mail and lingered to hear the gossip about the cigar-stand, it would be growing dark by the time I came home. The sun was gone; the frozen streets stretched long and blue before me; the lights were shining pale in kitchen windows, and I could smell the suppers cooking as I passed. Few people were abroad, and each one of them was hurrying toward a fire. The glowing stoves in the houses were like magnets. When one passed an old man, one could see nothing of his face but a red nose sticking out between a frosted beard and a long plush cap. The young men capered along with their hands in their pockets, and sometimes tried a slide on the icy sidewalk. The children, in their bright hoods and comforters, never walked, but always ran from the moment they left their door, beating their mittens against their sides. When I got as far as the Methodist Church, I was about halfway home. I can remember how glad I was when there happened to be a light in the church, and the painted glass window shone out at us as we came along the frozen street. In the winter bleakness a hunger for colour came over people, like the Laplander's craving for fats and sugar. Without knowing why, we used to linger on the sidewalk outside the church when the lamps were lighted early for choir practice or prayer-meeting, shivering and talking until our feet were like lumps of ice. The crude reds and greens and blues of that coloured glass held us there.

In the third section of the novel we lose sight of Ántonia almost completely. This section deals with Jim Burden at the University of Nebraska, his mild affair with Lina Lingard, one of the Swedish farm girls who has come to the city and set up as a dressmaker, and his decision to continue his studies at Harvard. Jim and his development provide the chief center of interest here, and one suspects that Miss Cather is drawing on her own experiences at the University of Nebraska. The high point of this section is an account of a performance of *Camille*, to which Jim takes Lina. The part of Marguerite was taken by a battered old actress, and in many other respects the performance lacked distinction, but for both Jim and Lina this performance of *Camille* by a rather run-down touring company in Lincoln, Nebraska, was one of the great and critical experiences of their lives.

In the fourth section Jim, going home from Harvard in the summer vacation, learns of Ántonia's fate. She had fallen in love with a railroad conductor and gone off to Denver to marry him: but he had not married her, for, unknown to her, he had already lost his job, and he ran off to Mexico leaving her pregnant. Ántonia goes back to her brother's farm subdued but determined to work once again on the land. Jim learns all the details, including the birth of Ántonia's baby, from Mrs. Steavens, who rents the Burdens' old farm. He goes out to see Antonia and finds her in the fields, shocking wheat: "She was thinner than I had ever seen her, and looked as Mrs. Steavens said, 'worked down,' but there was a new kind of strength in the gravity of her face, and her colour still gave her that look of deep-seated health and ardour. Still? Why, it flashed across me that though so much had happened in her life and in mine, she was barely twenty-four years old."

She tells him that she would always be miserable in a city. "I'd die of lonesomeness. I like to be where I know every stack and tree, and where all the ground is friendly." The Nebraska fields where she and Jim ran about as children now present themselves as the means of her salvation. And yet this rooting of herself in the American soil—a process hastened by her misfortune —is not achieved at the expense of repudiating her

Decline of the West

European past. They talk of her father. "He's been dead all these years," Antonia tells Jim, "and yet he is more real to me than almost anybody else. He never goes out of my life. I talk to him and consult him all the time. The older I grow, the better I know him and the more I understand him." This section ends on a note of hope:

As we walked homeward across the fields, the sun dropped and lay like a great golden globe in the low west. While it hung there, the moon rose in the east, as big as a cart-wheel, pale silver and streaked with rose colour, thin as a bubble or a ghost-moon. For five, perhaps ten minutes, the two luminaries confronted each other across the level land, resting on opposite edges of the world.

In that singular light every little tree and shock of wheat, every sunflower stalk and clump of snow-on-the-mountain, drew itself up high and pointed; the very clods and furrows in the fields seemed to stand up sharply. I felt the old pull of the earth, the solemn magic that comes out of those fields at nightfall. I wished I could be a little boy again, and that my way could end there.

Finally, Jim joins the company of Ántonia's friendly ghosts:

"I'll come back," I said earnestly, through the soft, intrusive darkness.

"Perhaps you will"—I felt rather than saw her smile. "But even if you don't, you're here, like my father. So I won't be lonesome."

As I went back alone over that familiar road, I could almost believe that a boy and girl ran along beside me, as our shadows used to do, laughing and whispering to each other in the grass.

57

Perhaps the book ought to have ended here, with Antonia left alone in the field in the gathering darkness. The concluding section, which redeems Antonia to a conventional happy ending, kills altogether that note of implicit tragedy that had been sounded in the earlier part of the novel. Yet the conclusion can be justified: it has an appropriate symbolic quality, and the return to Bohemia implied in Antonia's marriage to a Bohemian immigrant and raising a family who speak only Czech at home resolves an important aspect of the novel's theme.

The final section takes place twenty years later, when Jim returns to the scenes of his childhood and visits Ántonia. "I heard of her from time to time; that she married, very soon after I last saw her, a young Bohemian, a cousin of Anton Jellinek; that they were poor, and had a large family." When he visits her, surrounded by a large family, he can see at once that she has found her proper function as housewife and mother on a Nebraska farm:

I lay awake for a long while, until the slow-moving moon passed my window on its way up the heavens. I was thinking about Ántonia and her children; about Anna's solicitude for her, Ambrosch's grave affection, Leo's jealous, animal little love. That moment, when they all came tumbling out of the cave into the light, was a sight any man might have come far to see. Antonia had always been one to leave images in the mind that did not fade—that grew stronger with time. In my memory there was a succession of such pictures, fixed there like the old woodcuts of one's first primer: Antonia kicking her bare legs against the sides of

Decline of the West

my pony when we came home in triumph with our snake;
Ántonia in her black shawl and fur cap, as she stood by her
father's grave in the snowstorm; Antonia coming in with
her work-team along the evening skyline. She lent herself
to immemorial human attitudes which we recognize by
instinct as universal and true. I had not been mistaken. She
was a battered woman now, not a lovely girl; but she still
had that something which fires the imagination, could still
stop one's breath for a moment by a look or gesture that
somehow revealed the meaning in common things. She had
only to stand in the orchard, to put her hand on a little
crab tree and look up at the apples, to make you feel the
goodness of planting and tending and harvesting at last.
All the strong things of her heart came out in her body, that
had been so tireless in serving generous emotions.

It was no wonder that her sons stood tall and straight.
She was a rich mine of life, like the founders of early races.

Jim meets Ántonia's husband, a lively, humorous, de-
pendable Czech, a man more fitted by temperament for
the gay life of cities than life on a lonely farm.

I could see the little chap, sitting here every evening by
the windmill, nursing his pipe and listening to the silence;
the wheeze of the pump, the grunting of the pigs, an occasional squawking when the hens were disturbed by a rat.
It did rather seem to me that Cuzak had been made the
instrument of Antonia's special mission. This was a fine
life, certainly, but it wasn't the kind of life he had wanted
to live. I wondered whether the life that was right for one
was ever right for two!

Before he leaves, Jim walks out over the familiar
countryside:

59

This was the road over which Ántonia and I came on that night when we got off the train at Black Hawk and were bedded down in the straw, wondering children, being taken we knew not whither. I had only to close my eyes to hear the rumbling of the wagons in the dark, and to be again overcome by that obliterating strangeness. The feelings of that night were so near that I could reach out and touch them with my hand. I had the sense of coming home to myself, and of having found out what a little circle man's experience is. For Ántonia and for me, this had been the road of Destiny; had taken us to those early accidents of fortune which predetermined for us all that we can ever be. Now I understood that the same road was to bring us together again. Whatever we had missed, we possessed together the precious, the incommunicable past.

The symbolism seems a little uncertain at the conclusion. The final suggestion that this is the story of Jim and Ántonia and their relations is not really borne out by the story as it has developed. It begins as that, but later the strands separate until we have three main themes all going—the history of Ántonia, the history of Jim, and scenes of Nebraska life. It seems that the autobiographical impulse that redeemed Willa Cather from what she later considered the barren artfulness of *Alexander's Bridge* had its own dangers and was responsible for the abundance of interesting but not wholly dominated material which is to be found in *My Ántonia* as in *O Pioneers!*. These two novels are in many respects more alike than any other two of her books: both show vitality, liveliness, and a fine descriptive gift; both show a remarkable ability to project characters and incidents as symbols; but in both the variety of material is not fully integrated with the main theme, and autobiography or regional curiosity sometimes leads the story astray. A flawed novel full of life and interest and possessing a powerful emotional rhythm in spite of its imperfect structural pattern is not, however, a mean achievement, and *My Antonia* will long be read with pleasure and excitement.

One of Ours (1922) is the last of the series of novels in which Willa Cather drew on her own experiences to show life on the Nebraska plains; but, unlike *O Pioneers!* and *My Antonia,* here the story is one of frustration rather than fulfillment, and the hero finds himself only in escape from everything that life on the Nebraska plains stood for. In structure it is not unlike *The Song of the Lark:* in both novels the central character has aspirations which go far beyond anything which life in the local community has to offer. The emphasis in *One of Ours* is not, however, on the development of an artist, but on the gradual suffocation of the sensitive and maladjusted hero until he is liberated, ironically enough, by the first World War, in which he is finally killed.

The maladjusted hero has long been a commonplace of modern fiction, and Willa Cather shared with her age an interest in the conflict between the sensitive individual and the world of conventional routine. To this subject she brought her preoccupation with the impact of the American West on a European sensibility and the claims of the Old World on the New. We have seen how important this theme is in some of her earlier novels:

here she handles it rather differently. The tone adopted toward the American farming scene is less lyrical and more critical, and there is no character in the novel who finds salvation in the land.

Claude Wheeler, the hero, is nineteen years old when we meet him at the novel's opening, and it is soon clear that he is in some deep and unrealized sense at war with his environment. He is sent to a shoddy denominational college in Lincoln, Nebraska, instead of to the University of Nebraska, where he wants to go. In Lincoln he makes friends with the Erlichs, a cultured German family who represent the lively world of art and spontaneity of feeling so far removed from anything he has previously known. He does manage to enroll in one course at the University, a course in history, which moves and excites him and leads him to nourish ambitions which are never understood at home—not even by his thoughtful and sympathetic mother who responds to his moods and hopes and frustrations without fully realizing what the trouble is. Around Claude move also his humorous and self-confident father, his mechanically minded younger brother Ralph, his thin-blooded, dyspeptic, prohibitionist, elder brother Bayliss who has a farm implement business in the near-by town of Frankfort, and old Mahailey, the servant, faithful, illiterate, perceptive. Mr. Wheeler's decision to send Ralph off to Colorado to look after a newly acquired ranch there and put Claude in charge of the Nebraska ranch end Claude's hopes of further education and of warming himself in the glow provided by the society of people like the Erlichs. At the end of the first section of the book he finds himself trapped and feels himself betrayed.

This sounds like a conventional enough plot, and it is, as far as the action goes up to this point. But the groundwork for future interesting developments is laid. Bayliss and the world of thin-blooded preachers represent a menace whose real danger Claude is not to realize until it attacks him in a quite unexpected way. There are compensations in the rustic life which eventually turn out to be the most sinister dangers of all. We realize this when the themes laid down in the first section are taken up and developed in the second. But before we leave the first section something must be said about some of the characters and situations it presents.

Early in the book there is a conversation between Claude and the free-thinking, realistic, wholly unromantic Ernest Havel, who had come over as a small boy from Austria:

"What are you going to do after a while, Ernest? Do you mean to farm all your life?"

"Naturally. If I were going to learn a trade, I'd be at it before now. What makes you ask that?"

"Oh, I don't know! I suppose people must think about the future sometime. And you're so practical."

"The future, eh?" Ernest shut one eye and smiled. "That's a big word. After I get a place of my own and have a good start, I'm going home to see my old folks some winter. Maybe I'll marry a nice girl and bring her back."

"Is that all?"

"That's enough, if it turns out right, isn't it?"

"Perhaps. It wouldn't be for me. I don't believe I can

ever settle down to anything. Don't you feel that at this
rate there isn't much in it?"

"In what?"

"In living at all, going on as we do. What do we get out
of it? Take a day like this: you waken up in the morning and
you're glad to be alive; it's a good enough day for anything,
and you feel sure something will happen. Well, whether it's
a workday or a holiday, it's all the same in the end. At night
you go to bed—nothing has happened."

"But what do you expect? What can happen to you, except in your own mind? If I get through my work, and get
an afternoon off to see my friends like this, it's enough for
me."

"Is it? Well, if we've only got once to live, it seems like
there ought to be something—well, something splendid
about life, sometimes."

Ernest was sympathetic now. He drew nearer to Claude as
they walked along and looked at him sidewise with concern.
"You Americans are always looking for something outside
yourselves to warm you up, and it is no way to do. In old
countries, where not very much can happen to us, we know
that,—and we learn to make the most of little things."

"The martyrs must have found something outside themselves. Otherwise they could have made themselves comfortable with little things."

"Why, I should say they were the ones who had nothing
but their idea! It would be ridiculous to get burned at the
stake for the sensation. Sometimes I think the martyrs had
a good deal of vanity to help them along, too."

Claude thought Ernest had never been so tiresome. He
squinted at a bright object across the fields and said cut-
tingly, "The fact is, Ernest, you think a man ought to be
satisfied with his board and clothes and Sundays off, don't
you?"

Ernest laughed rather mournfully. "It doesn't matter much what I think about it; things are as they are. Nothing is going to reach down from the sky and pick a man up, I guess."

Claude muttered something to himself, twisting his chin about over his collar as if he had a bridle-bit in his mouth.

When Claude is put in charge of the farm, he loses some of his restlessness in hard work: "The new field he ploughed and drilled himself. He put a great deal of young energy into it, and buried a great deal of discontent in its dark furrows. Day after day he flung himself upon the land and planted it with what was fermenting in him, glad to be so tired at night that he could not think."

For characters in Miss Cather's earlier novels, this kind of activity had represented the way of salvation. But the pattern is different for Claude. However hard he worked in the spring and summer, the inactivity of the winter brought back his restlessness. A visit to Lincoln and the Erlichs over Thanksgiving renewed all his old discontents.

When the second Friday came round, he went to bid his friends good-bye and explained that he must be going home tomorrow. On leaving the house that night, he looked back at the ruddy windows and told himself that it was good-bye indeed, and not, as Mrs. Erlich had fondly said, *auf wiedersehen.* Coming here only made him more discontented with his lot; his frail claim on his kind of life existed no longer. He must settle down into something that was his own, take hold of it with both hands, no matter how grim it was. The next day, during his journey out through the bleak winter country, he felt that he was going deeper and deeper into reality.

Ernest Havel keeps telling Claude that farming is "the best life in the world,"—

But if you went to bed defeated every night, and dreaded to wake in the morning, then clearly it was too good a life for you. To be assured, at his age, of three meals a day and plenty of sleep, was like being assured of a decent burial. Safety, security; if you followed that reasoning out, then the unborn, those who would never be born, were the safest of all; nothing could happen to them.

Claude knew, and everybody else knew, seemingly, that there was something wrong with him. He had been unable to conceal his discontent. Mr. Wheeler was afraid he was one of those visionary fellows who make unnecessary difficulties for themselves and other people. Mrs. Wheeler thought the trouble with her son was that he had not yet found his Saviour. Bayliss was convinced that his brother was a moral rebel, that behind his reticence and his guarded manner he concealed the most dangerous opinions. The neighbours liked Claude, but they laughed at him, and said it was a good thing his father was well fixed. Claude was aware that his energy, instead of accomplishing something, was spent in resisting unalterable conditions, and in unavailing efforts to subdue his own nature. When he thought he had at last got himself in hand, a moment would undo the work of days; in a flash he would be transformed from a wooden post into a living boy. He would spring to his feet, turn over quickly in bed, or stop short in his walk, because the old belief flashed up in him with an intense kind of hope, an intense kind of pain,—the conviction that there was something splendid about life, if he could but find it!

Meanwhile, the dyspeptic Bayliss is running around with Gladys Farmer, "the best musician in Frankfort," a poor schoolteacher with a love of the arts and a habit of spending more money on pretty clothes and concerts than her neighbors thought she had a right to. Claude, who knows that Bayliss has nothing to offer Gladys but his money, and senses that Gladys has a vision something like his own and certainly quite incomprehensible to Bayliss, resents Gladys' acceptance of Bayliss' attentions, and on this note Book One ends:

Claude told himself that in so far as Gladys was concerned he could make up his mind to the fact that he had been "stung" all along. He had believed in her fine feelings; believed implicitly. Now he knew she had none so fine that she couldn't pocket them when there was enough to be gained by it. Even while he said these things over and over, his old conception of Gladys, down at the bottom of his mind, remained persistently unchanged. But that only made his state of feeling the more painful. He was deeply hurt,—and for some reason youth, when it is hurt, likes to feel itself betrayed.

The plot is given an interesting twist in Book Two, where Claude, finding no other outlet for his sensibility, persuades himself that he is in love with the pallid, religious Enid Royce and marries her, only to find that visiting preachers and the prohibitionist cause are more important to her than her husband, and that her prim religiosity sets an impassable barrier between them. Book Two, which is brief, ends with a grim honeymoon scene, and in Book Three the fortunes of Enid and Claude are pursued to the point where Enid leaves for

China to look after her seriously ill missionary sister there and Claude, hurt, bewildered, and more restless than ever, returns to his parents' house.

The religious theme runs strongly through the early sections of the novel: the gentle faith of Mrs. Wheeler, the unimaginative skepticism of Ernest Havel, the peevish asceticism of Bayliss, the calmly arrogant evangelism of Enid, the inefficient mediocrity of the denominational college at Lincoln—these all play their part in helping to isolate Claude, who is both skeptical and romantic, and enjoys the Bible and *Paradise Lost* as he enjoys Homer or Virgil. His marriage only emphasizes his loneliness, and the fact that the nonmaterial side of life is represented by such uncongenial forms at home makes him idealize more and more the life of art and European culture that he had caught a glimpse of at the Erlichs'. When war breaks out in Europe, therefore, Claude feels himself involved at once.

Meanwhile, Claude has been drawing closer to his mother, who responds to his moods and frustrations without fully understanding their origin. When the Germans move into France and threaten Paris, Claude and his mother pore over the article on Paris in the encyclopedia. Very deftly Miss Cather traces the impact of the war on American opinion, and she shows how Claude, in spite of his sympathy with the world of German culture represented by the Erlichs, comes to identify the threatened Paris with all that is valuable in the European spirit. Miss Cather holds the balance with considerable adroitness. While describing with obvious sympathy the growing opposition to Germany's behavior, she never allows the other Germany to be obscured, nor does she cover up the absurdity and cruelty of shallow patriots who persecuted their fellow citizens of German origin. But all this is described not in order to interpret America's reaction to the war but in order to show the development of Claude's attitude under the impact of these events. When America finally enters the war, Claude enlists, and after his training goes over to France with a commission. The war has finally thrown down the restricting walls of his environment, and he leaves for Europe in a spirit of high adventure.

Before he leaves he visits Gladys Farmer for the last time and finally admits his fears about her and Bayliss.

"I don't think I shall ever marry Bayliss," Gladys spoke in her usual low, round voice, but her quick breathing showed he had touched something that hurt. "I suppose I have used him. It gives a school-teacher a certain prestige if people think she can marry the rich bachelor of the town whenever she wants to. But I am afraid I won't marry him,—because you are the member of the family I have always admired."

Claude turned away to the window. "A fine lot I've been to admire," he muttered.

"Well, it's true, anyway. It was like that when we went to High School, and it's kept up. Everything you do always seems exciting to me."

Claude felt a cold perspiration on his forehead. He wished now that he had never come. "But that's it, Gladys. What *have* I ever done, except make one blunder after another?"

She came over to the window and stood beside him. "I don't know; perhaps it's by their blunders that one gets to know people,—by what they can't do. If you'd been like all the rest, you could have got on in their way. That was the one thing I couldn't have stood."

Claude was frowning out into the flaming garden. He had not heard a word of her reply. "Why didn't you keep me from making a fool of myself?" he asked in a low voice.

"I think I tried—once. Anyhow, it's all turning out better than I thought. You didn't get stuck here. You've found your place. You're sailing away. You've just begun."

"And what about you?"

She laughed softly. "Oh, I shall teach in the High School!"

Claude took her hands and they stood looking searchingly at each other in the swimming golden light that made everything transparent. He never knew exactly how he found his hat and made his way out of the house. He was only sure that Gladys did not accompany him to the door. He glanced back once, and saw her head against the bright window.

She stood there, exactly where he left her, and watched the evening come on, not moving, scarcely breathing. She was thinking how often, when she came downstairs, she would see him standing here by the window, or moving about in the dusky room, looking at last as he ought to look, —like his convictions and the choice he had made. She would never let this house be sold for taxes now. She would save her salary and pay them off. She could never like any other room so well as this. It had always been a refuge from Frankfort; and now there would be this vivid, confident figure, an image as distinct to her as the portrait of her grandfather upon the wall.

Gladys as a symbol of the woman of sensibility fighting a lone battle in an unsympathetic environment is

Decline of the West

not altogether successful. She is a mere bundle of literary conventions. But her reintroduction into the novel at this point shows a good sense of plotting: Claude goes to France to find what Gladys thinks she stands for.

The remarkable thing about the rest of the novel (nearly half is still to come) is that Miss Cather lets Claude find in France what he expected to find, without in any way softening the impact of the war scenes or describing the fighting as anything other than the wasteful and cruel business it actually was. The book ends with Claude's death, yet the ending is hardly tragic because any future for Claude after his experiences in France could only be anticlimax.

This latter part of the book is a small war novel in itself: it is in two parts, the first (Book Four of the novel) a description of the voyage across, and the second (Book Five) taking the story to its conclusion. Book Four, "The Voyage of the Anchises," is a remarkable piece of descriptive writing, done with vigor, liveliness, and a sharp eye for detail. It stands out from the novel as almost a short story in its own right—it could be read by itself without loss, and its relation to the main themes of the novel is of the most tenuous. Book Five, "Bidding the Eagles of the West Fly On," is Willa Cather's war novel —an unexpected piece of work to come from the author of *O Pioneers!* and *My Ántonia*.

Much of Book Five is simply the vivid war reporting of which we have had such a great deal in the years since the publication of *One of Ours*. Much of it is tedious and reflects attitudes of the time that now seem to us

71

naïve or untenable. One wonders where Miss Cather got her detailed and on the whole accurate knowledge of conditions on the Western Front—she must have collected information carefully from veterans. The sensibility at work here seems doggedly masculine and more conventional than that displayed in her other work. The inevitable emasculation of soldiers' dialogue and the presence of the unusual theme of Claude's pursuit of the European spirit in the midst of the trenches to some extent modifies the masculine sensibility and renders it unconvincing. It is the working out of this latter theme that enables Miss Cather to link up the farming novel with the war novel in *One of Ours*. Even so, the book is structurally broken-backed.

Claude has not been long in France before he meets a character who is to play the part that the Erlichs and, to a lesser extent, Gladys Farmer had played in the earlier part of the novel. This is Lieutenant David Gerhardt, an American who had studied the violin in Paris before the war, a not very convincing symbol of that combination of American ideals and European culture which is what Claude has been searching for. At least, Claude takes him to be such a symbol, although, with an effective touch of bitterness, Miss Cather makes clear that David Gerhardt is anything but that in his own eyes.

Gerhardt introduces Claude to islands of French civilization in the midst of the confusion and destruction of war, and these scenes are described with something of that lyrical tone Miss Cather had employed in depicting the Nebraska plains in *O Pioneers!* and *My Antonia:*

The next day was Claude's twenty-fifth birthday, and in honour of that event Papa Joubert produced a bottle of old Burgundy from his cellar, one of a few dozens he had laid in for great occasions when he was a young man.

During that week of idleness at Madame Joubert's, Claude often thought that the period of happy "youth," about which his old friend Mrs. Erlich used to talk, and which he had never experienced, was being made up to him now. He was having his youth in France. He knew that nothing like this would ever come again; the fields and woods would never again be laced over with this hazy enchantment. As he came up the village street in the purple evening, the smell of wood-smoke from the chimneys went to his head like a narcotic, opened the pores of his skin, and sometimes made the tears come to his eyes. Life had after all turned out well for him, and everything had a noble significance. The nervous tension in which he had lived for years now seemed incredible to him . . . absurd and childish, when he thought of it at all. He did not torture himself with recollections. He was beginning over again.

One night he dreamed that he was at home; out in the ploughed fields, where he could see nothing but the furrowed brown earth, stretching from horizon to horizon. Up and down it moved a boy, with a plough and two horses. At first he thought it was his brother Ralph; but on coming nearer, he saw it was himself,—and he was full of fear for this boy. Poor Claude, he would never, never get away; he was going to miss everything! While he was struggling to speak to Claude, and warn him, he awoke.

Willa Cather

"Bidding the Eagles of the West Fly On," for all its echoing of certain contemporary attitudes about the war, is full of incident and variety, the scenes alternating fairly regularly between the dirt and fatigue of the front on the one hand and conversations or meditations in the French countryside or in the homes of French families on the other. Miss Cather manages throughout it all to make Claude's sense of escape and achievement convincing without in any way playing down the horrors of war. At the end, both Claude and David Gerhardt are killed in a conventionally heroic episode. The novel returns at its conclusion to Nebraska and the two old women—Mrs. Wheeler and Mahailey—who work together in the farmhouse. The elegiac note here emerges clearly, but it does not obscure the resolution of the main theme: Claude Wheeler *did* escape, did find what he wanted even though it took a war to provide it for him. ("You'll admit it's a costly way of providing adventure for the young," Gerhardt had dryly remarked when Claude had tried to explain how the war had come to him as a liberation.) If he had returned, he would have had to face the same problems many times magnified.

In the dark months that followed, when human nature looked to her uglier than it had ever done before, those letters were Mrs. Wheeler's comfort. As she read the newspapers, she used to think about the passage of the Red Sea, in the Bible; it seemed as if the flood of meanness and greed had been held back just long enough for the boys to go over, and then swept down and engulfed everything that was left at home. When she can see nothing that has come of it all but evil, she reads Claude's letters over again and reassures herself; for him the call was clear, the cause was glorious. Never a doubt stained his bright faith. She divines so much that he did not write. She knows what to read into those short flashes of enthusiasm; how fully he must have found his life before he could let himself go so far—he, who was so afraid of being fooled! He died believing his own country better than it is, and France better than any country can ever be. And those were beautiful beliefs to die with. Perhaps it was as well to see that vision, and then to see no more. She would have dreaded the awakening,—she sometimes even doubts whether he could have borne at all that last, desolating disappointment. One by one the heroes of that war, the men of dazzling soldiership, leave prematurely the world they have come back to. Airmen whose deeds were tales of wonder, officers whose names made the blood of youth beat faster, survivors of incredible dangers,—one by one they quietly die by their own hand. Some do it in obscure lodging houses, some in their office, where they seemed to be carrying on their business like other men. Some slip over a vessel's side and disappear into the sea. When Claude's mother hears of these things, she shudders and presses her hands tight over her breast, as if she had him there. She feels as if God had saved him from some horrible suffering, some horrible end. For as she reads, she thinks those slayers of themselves were all so like him; they were the ones who had hoped extravagantly,—who in order to do what they did had to hope extravagantly, and to believe passionately. And they found they had hoped and believed too much. But one she knew, who could ill bear disillusion . . . safe, safe.

The irony here is obvious enough, but it is mellowed by the quietly elegiac note which surrounds it. Perhaps, after the liveliness and variety of the war scenes, it is too much to expect that the reader should be content to accept this atmosphere too long, and the muted rhythms of daily life on the farm hardly provide a forceful enough conclusion to this diversified story. Yet it is not difficult to see what Willa Cather is trying to do here: Claude went to Europe to try to solve an American problem, and it is proper to return at the end to the soil out of which that problem grew. In its final paragraph the images are deliberately and plangently domestic:

Mahailey, when they are alone, sometimes addresses Mrs. Wheeler as "Mudder"; "Now, Mudder, you go upstairs an' lay down an' rest yourself." Mrs. Wheeler knows that then she is thinking of Claude, is speaking for Claude. As they are working at the table or bending over the oven, something reminds them of him, and they think of him together, like one person: Mahailey will pat her back and say, "Never you mind, Mudder; you'll see your boy up yonder." Mrs. Wheeler always feels that God is near,—but Mahailey is not troubled by any knowledge of interstellar spaces, and for her He is nearer still,—directly overhead, not so very far above the kitchen stove.

One of Ours is a difficult novel to assess critically. There is considerable skill displayed in the individual scenes; some of the episodes are done with a keen reportorial eye and at the same time a fine sense of symbolic detail; the book is rarely dull or awkward or commonplace. Yet we cannot help feeling that the combination of impulses out of which this book grew were never fully reconciled. In one of its aspects the novel is a mere patriotic exercise, reflecting the one occasion when Miss Cather was deflected by the pressure of contemporary events from the pursuit of her personal vision. The personal vision is also there, however, for she tried to make a war novel into an exploration of one of her favorite themes—the decline of the pioneering age and the plight of the imaginative hero in an increasingly narrow and self-satisfied civilization. The war was not, perhaps, the proper subject to use, even in part, as a vehicle for the presentation of this theme, and for all the adroitness with which its various elements are manipulated, *One of Ours* remains an uneven and a puzzling novel.

A Lost Lady followed *One of Ours* in 1923. It is a short novel, more intimate in tone and more restricted in scope than any Willa Cather had previously written. The setting is Sweet Water, Colorado, just after hopes for its future as an important and expanding town on the Burlington Railroad had begun to fade, and this atmosphere of fading hope provides an effective background for the story of Mrs. Forrester, the lost lady. The pattern of rising achievement which lies behind her earlier novels of the West has given way to one of frustration. Maladjustment and frustration had been in part the theme of *One of Ours,* but there the personal frustration had not been set against the decline of a community. The history of Sweet Water is almost that of a ghost town—the great Western dream in reverse:

All this while the town of Sweet Water was changing. Its future no longer looked bright. Successive crop failures had broken the spirit of the farmers. . . . The Forresters now

77

had fewer visitors. The Burlington was "drawing in its horns," as people said, and the railroad officials were not stopping off at Sweet Water so often,—were more inclined to hurry past a town where they had sunk money that would never come back.

Captain Forrester was "a railroad man, a contractor, who had built hundreds of miles of road for the Burlington," married to a beautiful and lively wife twenty-five years his junior. At first they lived in their Sweet Water home only a few months out of each year, but that was enough to enable the Forresters to establish their position in the town as representatives of a more gracious and aristocratic way of living than the rough natives of the place were accustomed to. Mrs. Forrester, universally admired and even worshiped, presided with charm, beauty, and gaiety over a house that regularly entertained distinguished or wealthy visitors from the East. Even the uncouth town boys felt the impact of her graciously aristocratic presence (aristocratic without being in the least snobbish or patronizing), except for the unscrupulous, jealous, swaggering Ivy Peters, soon to develop into a cunning and crooked lawyer.

After Mr. Forrester's "terrible fall with his horse in the mountains," he and his wife retired permanently to Sweet Water, and the main part of the story is concerned with Mrs. Forrester's decline from the charming hostess in a lively community to the desperate, trapped woman making every endeavor to escape from the narrow and increasingly shabby environment to which her destiny has confined her. Her decline is hastened by her husband's impoverishment as a result of the failure of a savings bank in Denver in which he was interested: Captain Forrester insisted on using all his own remaining resources in order to pay the depositors—all working men, who knew his name and trusted him—a hundred cents on the dollar, even though the other bank officers wanted to share the loss with the depositors and refused to follow his example. The result was that the depositors did not lose a cent, but the Forresters were henceforth poor people.

The remainder of the book traces the decline of Mrs. Forrester, as she grows increasingly desperate at the thought of being permanently cut off from the lively social world outside. Even before the bank failure she had been restive under the increasingly restricted social life of Sweet Water and had had an affair with Frank Ellinger, "a bachelor of forty, six feet two, with long straight legs, fine shoulders, and a figure that still permitted his white waistcoat to button without a wrinkle under his conspicuously well-cut dinner coat." Ellinger was a dashing bachelor with a "dangerous" reputation, and his occasional visits to the Forresters at Sweet Water became for Mrs. Forrester a symbol of her escape to a life of romance and excitement. When the Captain went off to Denver to see about the bank failure, Ellinger came to Sweet Water and spent the night with Mrs. Forrester.

The Captain has a series of strokes, and Mrs. Forrester shows more and more signs of strain as he becomes virtually helpless, and she has to devote her life to caring for him. She goes to pieces on hearing of Frank Ellinger's marriage, consoles herself even more frequently with brandy, and finally takes up with the unspeakable Ivy Peters, symbol of all that is coarse and cunning in the younger "generation of shrewd young men." Mr. Forrester dies at last, and at this point Niel Herbert, the young man through whose eyes the story has been presented (though it is not told in the first person, like *My Ántonia*), leaves Sweet Water permanently, and we lose sight of the lost lady. Many years later Niel meets an old Sweet Water friend and learns from him that Mrs. Forrester had married again—"a rich, cranky old Englishman"—and thus had been restored to the world of wealth and gaiety, though presumably at a price; his friend also tells him that she had died three years before.

Such a bare summary of the plot might suggest that *A Lost Lady* is essentially the story of the degeneration of a socially minded lady who is condemned to pass her days in a poor and rough community. Miss Cather's main interest, however, is less in the study of degeneration than in the exploration and presentation of those ambiguities and paradoxes of human character than make it possible for someone like Mrs. Forrester to be at once the epitome of aristocratic grace, kindness, and understanding, and a vulgarian who will do anything— deceive her husband, make advances to coarse and unprincipled young men—to get some excitement out of life. At home her relations with her husband were ideal. He was devoted to her in an old-fashioned, courtly way, and she behaved to him with tenderness and understanding. This broken old railroad builder, no longer, since his accident, able to go out into the great world where he had once cut such an impressive figure, preserved in his daily living a formal courtesy, a simple yet almost ritualistic dignity, to which she responded with apparent love and appreciation:

Curiously enough, it was as Captain Forrester's wife that she most interested Niel, and it was in her relation to her husband that he most admired her. Given her other charming attributes, her comprehension of a man like the railroad-builder, her loyalty to him, stamped her more than anything else. That, he felt, was quality; something that could never become worn or shabby; steel of Damascus. His admiration of Mrs. Forrester went back to that, just as, he felt, she herself went back to it. He rather liked the stories, even the spiteful ones, about the gay life she led in Colorado, and the young men she kept dangling about her every winter. He sometimes thought of the life she might have been living ever since he had known her,—and the one she had chosen to live. From that disparity, he believed, came the subtlest thrill of her fascination. She mocked outrageously at the proprieties she observed, and inherited the magic of contradictions.

This was before he had discovered her affair with Ellinger. One summer morning, when the Captain is away in Denver, Niel comes up to the Forrester house to lay a bunch of roses on Mrs. Forrester's bedroom window sill; and behind the shutters he hears "a woman's soft laughter" answered by the fat and lazy laugh of Ellinger. Niel is horrified and outraged.

"Lilies that fester," he muttered, *"lilies that fester smell far worse than weeds."*

Grace, variety, the lovely voice, the sparkle of fun and fancy in those dark eyes; all this was nothing. It was not a moral scruple she had outraged, but an aesthetic ideal. Beautiful women, whose beauty meant more than it said . . . was their brilliancy always fed by something coarse and concealed? Was that their secret?

But Niel returns to be fascinated by the lady's charm and vitality. Before he leaves for Boston, he calls on the Forresters. The Captain has recently had his first stroke and moves slowly and heavily, but both he and his wife entertain with spirit and charm, drinking to his future as an architect.

Captain Forrester rose heavily, with the aid of his cane, and went into the dining-room. He brought back the decanter and filled three glasses with ceremony. Lifting his glass, he paused, as always, and blinked.

"Happy days!"

"Happy days!" echoed Mrs. Forrester, with her loveliest smile, "and every success to Niel!"

Both the Captain and his wife came to the door with him, and stood there on the porch together, where he had so often seen them stand to speed the parting guest. He went down the hill touched and happy. As he passed over the bridge his spirits suddenly fell. Would that chilling doubt always lie in wait for him, down there in the mud, where he had thrown his roses one morning?

He burned to ask her one question, to get the truth out of her and set his mind at rest: What did she do with all her exquisiteness when she was with a man like Ellinger? Where did she put it away? And having put it away, how could she recover herself, and give one—give even him— the sense of tempered steel, a blade that could fence with anyone and never break?

Decline of the West

Niel returns to Sweet Water two years later to find the Forresters sadly declined in style of living and Ivy Peters increasingly influential with Mrs. Forrester. Peters is a symbol of the decline of the West, and, as this is the story of the frustration of Western dreams, his increasing significance as the novel develops is thoroughly appropriate:

The Old West had been settled by dreamers, great-hearted adventurers who were unpractical to the point of magnificence; a courteous brotherhood, strong in attack but weak in defence, who could conquer but could not hold. Now all the vast territory they had won was to be at the mercy of men like Ivy Peters, who had never dared anything, never risked anything. They would drink up the mirage, dispel the morning freshness, root out the great brooding spirit of freedom, the generous, easy life of the great land-holders. The space, the colour, the princely carelessness of the pioneer they would destroy and cut up into profitable bits, as the match factory splinters the primeval forest. All the way from the Missouri to the mountains this generation of shrewd young men, trained to petty economies by hard times, would do exactly what Ivy Peters had done when he drained the Forrester marsh.

Niel, on the other hand, is that characteristic Cather figure, the sensitive young man who reads the poets alone of an evening and eventually goes East to an appropriate profession. As the story is told from his point of view, although not in his words, it is important that he should be endowed with the proper sensitivity. Miss Cather, therefore, gives us glimpses of his education, tells of his discovery of Byron, *Tom Jones, Wilhelm Meister,* his reading of Montaigne and Ovid. Her description of the effect of his reading on him reminds one of Jim Burden (of *My Ántonia*) at the University of Nebraska:

He was eavesdropping upon the past, being let into the great world that had plunged and glittered and sumptuously sinned long before little Western towns were dreamed of. Those rapt evenings beside the lamp gave him a long perspective, influenced his conception of the people about him, made him know just what he wished his own relations with these people to be.

But it is Ivy Peters and his kind who remain in the West and to whom Mrs. Forrester turns in her desperate attempt to restore her fortunes. The Captain, growing ever more physically helpless, retains his perfect courtesy and dignity to the end, although, as is made clear, he has known all along of his wife's affair with Ellinger. After his return Niel remains in Sweet Water until the Captain's death and is able to observe the fine courtliness that persists in the relationship of the Forresters to each other, in spite of Mrs. Forrester's shady relations with such characters as Peters:

He had time to think of many things; of himself and of his old friends here. He had noticed that often when Mrs. Forrester was about her work, the Captain would call to her, "Maidy, Maidy," and she would reply, "Yes, Mr. Forrester," from wherever she happened to be, but without coming to him,—as if she knew that when he called to her in that tone he was not asking for anything. He wanted to know if she were near, perhaps; or, perhaps, he merely liked to call her name and hear her answer. The longer Niel was with Captain Forrester in those peaceful closing days of his life, the more he felt that the Captain knew his wife better even than she knew herself; and that, knowing her, he,—to use one of his own expressions,—valued her.

Mrs. Forrester's story is in some way bound up with "the end of the road-making West." Sweet Water did not become what it should have become; and Captain Forrester, his career as a railroad contractor cut short by an accident which is seen as the novel unfolds to be symbolic in its implications, is unable to provide for his young and lively wife the atmosphere of liveliness amid abundance which she was born for. The future is in the hands of the Ivy Peterses of America, and, since they represent progress, it is to them that the Mrs. Forresters have to turn. It is a desperate choice, however—indicated by the fact that during the period of her association with Peters, Mrs. Forrester takes more and more to drink. Niel passes the final judgment:

This was the very end of the road-making West; the men who had put plains and mountains under the iron harness were old; some were poor, and even the successful ones were hunting for rest and a brief reprieve from death. It was already gone, that age; nothing could ever bring it back. The taste and smell and song of it, the visions those men had seen in the air and followed,—these he had caught in a kind of afterglow in their own faces,—and this would always be his.

It was what he most held against Mrs. Forrester; that she was not willing to immolate herself, like the widow of all these great men, and die with the pioneer period to which she belonged; that she preferred life on any terms.

In the end she gets life on any terms, and we get our last glimpse of her with her rich and cranky old husband in Buenos Aires.

A Lost Lady is one of the most perfectly modulated of Willa Cather's novels. The central theme—the degeneration of Mrs. Forrester—is artfully linked to the background theme of the decline of the pioneering West. In Miss Cather's novels from *O Pioneers!* to *A Lost Lady* we can see the rise and fall of the pioneering ideal. The characters and situations of her earlier novels are set against a rising, and ultimately successful, pioneering effort, whereas in some degree in *One of Ours* and more obviously in *A Lost Lady* characters and situations develop against a background of declining vigor and increasing ordinariness and stereotyping. Alexandra Bergson and Antonia Shimerda found themselves in the heroic taming of the Nebraska plains; Marian Forrester lost herself in the emptying and vulgarizing process that followed. For all her fascination with and love for the American scene, Willa Cather had learned from the Populists to be suspicious of modern America. Her bitter remarks on the younger generation, who brought petty commercial and financial cunning to the dreams of their fathers, run right through her books about the West and can be put beside that disillusioned picture of America after the First World War which we find at the end of *One of Ours*.

CHAPTER 4

The Claims of History

THE EXPANSIVENESS of such novels as *O Pioneers!* and *My Ántonia* gradually gives way, in Miss Cather's work, to more concentrated novels of more limited scope. *A Lost Lady*, though it still has something of the western background, is focused throughout on a single character. In *The Professor's House*, which followed in 1925, the scope is similarly restricted. The novel is essentially the study of a middle-aged professor wrestling with his own sensitivities on the one hand and his family responsibilities on the other, but, interwoven with the professor's story and acting as a catalyst in projecting that story, is the story of Tom Outland, the brilliant, unconventional student who had been killed in the early days of the first World War. In both Tom Outland and the professor Miss Cather is exploring certain phases of sensibility, aspects of character which in some degree and at some time are bound to come in conflict with the demands of the conventional world.

We can trace the growth of this interest in the earlier novels. To some extent, it is present in *Alexander's Bridge*, but it gives way in the pioneering novels to

87

sturdier themes, emerging there only in incidental characters, until we see it again more fully revealed in Claude of *One of Ours*. *The Professor's House* is Miss Cather's first full-length treatment of a theme which has become so important in the twentieth-century novel, the first of her novels which links her, however tenuously, to what might be called the modern novel of sensibility so successfully practiced in England by Virginia Woolf and still very much alive. Not that there is any real resemblance between Miss Cather and Mrs. Woolf in attitude or technique—their art had very different foundations; but the exploration of individual sensitivity, so central in Virginia Woolf's fiction, does come to be one of Willa Cather's main interests at this stage in her career.

Willa Cather seems to have had a *mystique* about professors: we can see something of it in the picture of Gaston Cleric, the "brilliant and inspiring young scholar" in the third book of *My Antonia*, and in the brief but enthusiastic account of the history professor in *One of Ours* for whom Claude wrote a thesis on Jeanne d'Arc. *The Professor's House* has for its hero Professor Godfrey St. Peter, author of *Spanish Adventurers in North America*, intelligent, sensitive, unconventional, and, at the time the book opens, recently the recipient of an Oxford prize for history. The prize has enabled the professor, on his wife's suggestion, to build a fine new house. He does not, however, share his wife's enthusiasm for the new house, preferring the shabby attic of the old house to the glories that await him in the new. In that study his great work was written, and it is associated with all that he considers most worth-while in his own life. The book opens with his reluctant move from the old house to the new and his decision to continue renting the old house so that he can continue to use his beloved study.

At this crisis in his life—for we first see him at that dangerous period of middle age when restlessness and an undefined dissatisfaction begin to haunt him—he feels himself more and more removed from the normal world of bright and polite social behavior, and although there is no breach with his wife it is made clear that his increasing lack of interest in the world in which she moves is drawing him apart from her. His series of volumes on the Spaniards in North America (which on publication were looked upon with suspicion by conventional academic historians, but which have eventually won him fame among a limited number of initiates who understand what he was doing) evidence an interest in the adventurous side of history and are also bound up with his interest in Tom Outland. Outland had descended on the professor many years before as a young man with an unconventional New Mexico background. His full story is told in Book Two of the novel, where we learn that he had been orphaned in infancy and had worked as a railroad callboy in Pardee, New Mexico, and then, with his friend Rodney Blake, as a cowboy for a big New Mexico cattle company. It was while riding the range that he and Rodney had discovered, on the top of a long unexplored mesa, "a little city of stone," the perfectly preserved home of long-vanished pueblo Indians. He had fallen in love with this town in the cliffs and with Rodney Blake had explored it passionately and lovingly. He had spent some time in Washington trying to get officials of the Smithsonian Institution interested in excavating it, but without success. On his return from Washington he found that Blake, despairing of Washington interest and misunderstanding the nature of Outland's interest, had sold the pottery in which Cliff City (as they called it) abounded for a handsome sum to a German entrepreneur. Outland's fury at finding what his friend had done (though it had been done with the best of intentions and the money had been deposited in the bank in Outland's name) led to the separation of the friends, and Outland eventually turned up at the professor's university seeking an education. He had already received some education, including a good grounding in Latin, from a Catholic priest who had been interested in him.

In the first part of the novel, however, all we know of Tom Outland is that he had appeared from the unknown, had been befriended by the professor and his family, and had turned out a brilliant physicist. He had invented the Outland vacuum, which "revolutionized aviation." On the outbreak of the first World War he had quixotically gone off to Europe to enlist in the French Foreign Legion. There he was killed before he was thirty years old and, having before his departure become engaged to the professor's elder daughter Rosamond, left her in his will everything that he owned. It was later realized that the Outland vacuum, if properly exploited, would make a fortune, and the flamboyant and able Louie Marsellus, himself an electrical engineer, who fell in love with Rosamond and married her, investigated the commercial possibilities of the patent which now belonged to his wife and made a great financial success of it.

The professor's younger daughter, Kathleen, more sensitive and much less rich than Rosamond, is married to Scott McGregor, a young journalist who manages to earn a moderate income by writing, among other things, a daily "prose poem" for the popular press. Being a sensitive and ambitious young man, he is disgusted with his way of earning a living and ashamed at his own facility in turning out such stuff. His brother-in-law Louie Marsellus, assured, generous, and completely the extrovert, inevitably arouses Scott's hostility, while Kathleen resents her elder sister's wealth and arrogant bearing, a resentment reciprocated by Rosamond who feels that her sister and brother-in-law privately mock her own and her husband's social pretensions.

The professor is not unaware of the tension that exists between his two daughters. His own favorite is Kathleen, while his wife seems to take a greater interest in the flashier Rosamond and her smooth and charming husband, who adores his mother-in-law and plays up to her on every possible occasion. All are haunted by the memory of Tom Outland, whose name flits like a disturbing ghost through their conversation. Marsellus is building a pretentious country house and announces his decision to call it "Outland," in recognition of Tom's achievement and to show that he is aware of the source of his fortune. This decision, applauded by Rosamond and by Mrs. St. Peter, outrages the McGregors

(McGregor, not Marsellus, had been Tom's friend) and is met coldly by the professor. We also learn that it was the professor's growing affection for Tom Outland that first aroused his wife's jealous sense of something dividing her from her husband. Now that there is an undefinable but unmistakable distance between the professor and his wife, we become increasingly aware of how the professor's interest in the Spanish Southwest, his feeling about his historical research, and his attitude toward Outland have combined to set him apart and to produce the crisis in the midst of which we find him when the book opens.

The book as a whole is the story of the development and resolution of this crisis, but it is also Tom Outland's story, and the fact that Miss Cather can make these two stories one with no sense of strain or structural artificiality is a tribute to the maturity of her art at this stage. Tom Outland's story, in turn, is bound up with the Southwest, with the Cliff Dwellers, and with that feeling for the impact of the past on the present which was strong in Miss Cather and which we first see in the Cliff Dweller scenes in *The Song of the Lark*. Thus the professor and Tom are linked to each other by a sensitivity to history—not academic history (which does not admit of this kind of sensitivity), but history conceived as a series of past human adventures whose implications reverberate excitingly into the present. Tom's joy in discovering and investigating Cliff City is the same kind of joy that the professor found in writing his *Spanish Adventurers in North America*. Indeed, he had gone with Tom on a journey of discovery in the Southwest using

The Claims of History

Tom's experiences as a guide in identifying places referred to in the journals of old Spanish explorers.

The new house threatens to cut the professor off from his past, from that period of his life when his daughters were children, when he was thoroughly *en rapport* with his family, when Tom Outland was a daily visitor to his home, and when he was engaged in the exciting task of getting his history under way.

"Godfrey," his wife had gravely said one day, when she detected an ironical turn in some remark he made about the new house, "is there something you would rather have done with that money than to have built a house with it?

"Nothing, my dear, nothing. If with that cheque I could have bought back the fun I had writing my history, you'd never have got your house. But one couldn't get that for twenty thousand dollars. The great pleasures don't come so cheap. There is nothing else, thank you."

The professor refuses to allow the dressmaker to remove from his old study the dress forms which she had kept there for so many years and on which so often his daughters' new party dresses had been left overnight. He keeps the shabby attic room with all its old properties as a refuge from the implications of his new house and from the brittle claims of society, a place in which to work and meditate and be alone and be himself. This sounds a tawdry enough piece of business, with its suggestions of the gloomy romantic hero or of the self-conscious Faustus in his study—but as Miss Cather handles it the theme emerges freshly and convincingly. She manipulates the professor's relations with his family very adroitly, refusing to allow herself the obvious device of a clear-cut distinction between sympathetic characters of perception and sensitivity and unsympathetic characters who lead a life of cheerful social insensitivity. Mrs. St. Peter is unsympathetic neither to the reader nor to the professor, and Louie Marsellus becomes more attractive as the book progresses. But in a sense the characters are all judged by their relation to the dead Tom Outland, and that is the principal reason why the McGregors emerge as in some undefined way superior to the Marselluses and why the professor remains an isolated figure whose isolation continues to increase until the conclusion of the story puts it suddenly but not improbably on a new basis.

Book One of *The Professor's House* is entitled "The Family" and explores the professor's relation to his wife, daughters, and sons-in-law. It concludes with the departure of Mrs. St. Peter and her daughter and son-in-law for a holiday in France; it was Louie's plan, and he is paying for everything. The professor has been warmly invited by Louie to make one of the party, but, to Louie's genuine disappointment, he refuses, finding himself unable to join in that kind of jaunt:

That night, after he was in bed, St. Peter tried in vain to justify himself in his inevitable refusal. He liked Paris, and he liked Louie. But one couldn't do one's own things in another person's way; selfish or not, that was the truth. Besides, he would not be needed. He could trust Louie to take every care of Lillian [his wife], and nobody could please her more than her son-in-law. . . . Many people admired her, but Louie more than most. That worldliness, that willingness to get the most out of occasions and people, which had developed so strongly in Lillian in the last few years, seemed to Louie as natural and proper as it seemed unnatural to Godfrey. It was an element that had always been in Lillian, and as long as it resulted in mere fastidiousness, was not a means to an end, St. Peter had liked it, too. He knew it was due to this worldliness, even more than to the fact that his wife had a little money of her own, that she and his daughters had never been drab and a little pathetic, like some of the faculty women. They hadn't much, but they were never absurd. They never made shabby compromises. If they couldn't get the right thing, they went without. Usually they had the right thing, and it got paid for, somehow. He couldn't say they were extravagant; the old house had been funny and bare enough, but there were no ugly things in it.

With his family away, the professor moves into the old house and more or less lives in the study. His plans are to spend the summer editing and annotating the diary kept by Tom Outland when he was investigating Cliff City. His meditations on Outland in the lonely house as he prepares to work on the diary provide Miss Cather with a perfect transition to "Tom Outland's Story," which occupies Book Two.

Earlier in the novel Scott McGregor makes a significant remark to his father-in-law. "You know, Tom isn't very real to me any more. Sometimes I think he was just a—a glittering idea." He had become "a glittering idea" to his friend McGregor; to Louie Marsellus, who had never met him, he was an adored name and the source of a fortune; to Mrs. St. Peter he was someone who had separated her in some degree from her husband: only Professor St. Peter himself remained to cherish Outland's memory, and as time went on Outland becomes a part of the professor's own history. Marsellus once suggested that he should settle some of Outland's money on the professor, since Outland had owed so much to him, but when Rosamond brings this message from her husband to her father, he repudiates the suggestion fiercely:

"Once and for all, Rosamond, understand that he owed me no more than I owed him. . . . In a lifetime of teaching, I've encountered just one remarkable mind; but for that, I'd consider my good years largely wasted. And there can be no question of money between me and Tom Outland. I can't explain just how I feel about it, but it would somehow damage my recollections of him, would make that episode in my life commonplace like everything else. And that would be a great loss to me. I'm purely selfish in refusing your offer; my friendship with Outland is the one thing I will not have translated into the vulgar tongue."

By the time we reach Book Two, therefore, the professor has become in some sense identified with Outland, and the story of Outland's life is part of the professor's own background.

"Tom Outland's Story" is set in the New Mexico landscape, and description of natural scenery is employed as an almost lyrical background to the boy's adventures. That background helps to explain not only Tom, but also the quality of the professor's feeling for history. The style of this part of the narrative is simple and swinging (it is supposed to be Tom's own words, the professor's recollection of the story Tom had told him). The first description of Cliff City gives some idea of the unpretentious but effective prose:

It was beautifully proportioned, that tower, swelling out to a larger girth a little above the base, then growing slender again. There was something symmetrical and powerful about the swell of the masonry. The tower was the fine thing that held all the jumble of houses together and made them mean something. It was red in colour, even on that grey day. In sunlight it was the colour of winter oak-leaves. A fringe of cedars grew along the edge of the cavern, like a garden. They were the only living things. Such silence and stillness and repose—immortal repose. That village sat looking down into the canyon with the calmness of eternity. The falling snow-flakes, sprinkling the piñons, gave it a special kind of solemnity. I can't describe it. It was more like sculpture than anything else. I knew at once that I had come upon the city of some extinct civilization, hidden away in this inaccessible mesa for centuries, preserved in the dry air and almost perpetual sunlight like a fly in amber, guarded by the cliffs and the river and the desert.

There is "the glory and the freshness of a dream" about much of this writing, which describes history impinging concretely on the mind of a naïve and enthusiastic youngster. Tom actually experienced what the professor has tried to distill in his writings:

One thing we knew about these people; they hadn't built their town in a hurry. Everything proved their patience and deliberation. The cedar joists had been felled with stone axes and rubbed smooth with sand. The little poles that

97

lay across them and held up the clay floor of the chamber above, were smoothly polished. The door lintels were carefully fitted (the doors were stone slabs held in place by wooden bars fitted into hasps). The clay dressing that covered the stone walls was tinted, and some of the chambers were frescoed in geometrical patterns, one color laid on another. In one room was a painted border, little tents, like Indian tepees, in brilliant red.

But the really splendid thing about our city, the thing that made it delightful to work there, and must have made it delightful to live there, was the setting. The town hung like a bird's nest in the cliff, looking off into the box canyon below, and beyond into the wide valley we called Cow Canyon, facing an ocean of clear air. A people who had the hardihood to build there, and who lived day after day looking down upon such grandeur, who came and went by those hazardous trails, must have been, as we often told each other, a fine people. But what had become of them? What catastrophe had overwhelmed them?

In Book Three of the novel we return to the professor. He is sitting in his old study reflecting on his own past. "He had had two romances: one of the heart, which had filled his life for many years, and a second of the mind—of the imagination. Just when the morning brightness of the world was wearing off for him, along came Outland and brought him a kind of second youth." Through Outland, he reflects, "he had been able to experience afresh things that had grown dull with use." Outland was responsible for the fact that "the last four volumes of *The Spanish Adventurers* were more simple and inevitable than· those that went before." He becomes the symbol of the professor's attitude to history.

The Claims of History

We learn of the professor's holidays in Europe, youthful trips to France and later expeditions to Spain, and these become linked in his and the reader's mind with his journeys in the American Southwest, to provide a background of warmth and color to his speculations about civilization. Here, as later in *Death Comes for the Archbishop,* Miss Cather takes her old conflicting interests in the American West and in European culture and fuses them in a new way. In her earlier novels, a character had to escape from one to achieve the other; but among the Indian and Spanish remains of the Southwest the conflict is resolved.

Meditating over his past alone in the old house the professor feels himself more and more detached from life, even from his own life. "He did not regret his life, but he was indifferent to it. It seemed to him like the life of another person." A conviction seizes him that he is near the end of his life, though his doctor assures him that there is nothing the matter with him. He falls asleep on his study couch with the gas fire lit, and a storm blows out the flame of the fire and slams the window shut. He realizes vaguely what has happened and knows that the room is filling with gas. "The thing to do was to get up and open the window. But suppose he did not get up—? How far was a man required to exert himself against accident?" He falls asleep but is discovered in time by Augusta, the sewing woman, who comes in to get the keys to open the new house, for the family is coming home from France.

The professor recovers himself in a conversation with Augusta, a practical, unimaginative woman, "seasoned and sound and on the solid earth . . . and, for all her matter-of-factness and hard-handedness, kind and loyal." Sitting quietly with Augusta, he thinks again of his past life, "trying to see where he had made his mistake."

Perhaps the mistake was merely in an attitude of mind. He had never learned to live without delight. And he would have to learn to, just as, in a Prohibition country, he supposed he would have to learn to live without sherry. Theoretically he knew that life is possible, may be even pleasant, without joy, without passionate griefs. But it had never occurred to him that he might have to live like that.

His reluctance to meet his returning family, to become involved in a domestic and social pattern again, continues, but as a result of his involuntary near-suicide a change comes over his attitude, which enables him to face the arrival of the "Berengaria," bringing his wife and the Marselluses back across the Atlantic, without anxiety.

His temporary release from consciousness seemed to have been beneficial. He had let something go—and it was gone: something very precious, that he could not consciously have relinquished, probably. He doubted whether his family would ever realize that he was not the same man they had said good-bye to; they would be too happily preoccupied with their own affairs. If his apathy hurt them, they could not possibly be so much hurt as he had been already. At least, he felt the ground under his feet. He thought he knew where he was, and that he could face with fortitude the *Berengaria* and the future.

The Claims of History

So the book concludes. It is a novel which sometimes barely avoids tawdry romantic situations and a too neat pairing off of introverts and extroverts. But they *are* avoided. The professor's intellectual and imaginative qualities are linked to the life of action through the subject of his historical researches (which are themselves bound up with his character) and his association with Tom Outland. His growing aloofness fits none of the formulas of the romantic hero, while the use made of Outland's early life and his exploration of Cliff City gives a wholly original tone to the story. The full meaning of the professor's crisis and its resolution is never overtly examined, and a note of deliberate mystery remains to the end. The novel is symbolic in a way in which *O Pioneers!* and *My Ántonia* are not, though these earlier novels have their own kind of symbolism. In some respects it is closer to *Alexander's Bridge* than any of the intervening novels, but it has more substance and more conviction than that early work. The pioneering novels and even such a small-scale affair as *A Lost Lady* were relatively rough-hewn works; *The Professor's House* shows Miss Cather moving toward a more delicate kind of art.

Willa Cather's next novel was the brief and curious *My Mortal Enemy*, published in 1926. In tone and scope it is reminiscent of *A Lost Lady*, but it lacks the clear surface and the firm control of the earlier work. It is the story of Myra Driscoll, who eloped from the home of her wealthy great-uncle, who was bringing her up, to marry Oswald Henshawe and as a result was cut off by her great-uncle without a penny. Oswald made a very moderate income as a businessman in New York, but when he and his wife were getting on in years he lost his job, and they moved to the West Coast in search of work. They end up at a poor lodging house in San Francisco, and Myra dies in poverty and bitterness, having turned against the man for whom she had sacrificed a fortune.

The story is told in the first person by a niece of an old friend of Myra's, who recalls her aunt's stories of Myra's brilliant youth and of her elopement and then gives an account of her own experiences with the Henshawes. The character of Myra is the story's principal interest: she is charming, brilliant, and generous, yet jealous and dominating. As she grows older she grows more jealous and more resentful, until at the end, forgetful of the happy times she and her husband had spent together in their relatively prosperous days, she feels that in eloping she had made the wrong decision, that her great-uncle had been right after all, and that her husband has become her mortal enemy. This study of the degeneration of a character lacks conviction partly because we are not given an adequate knowledge of Myra before the change sets in, partly because the incidents employed to illustrate her character are too often and too obviously contrived, and partly because of a melodramatic atmosphere hanging about the novel with no particular function to serve.

The theme is interesting enough, suggesting at times Maupassant and at times Flaubert, but Miss Cather here displays neither Maupassant's ironic realism nor Flau-

bert's meticulous skill in probing the sordidness underlying frustrated romanticism. The tone of chatty
reminiscence in which the story is told is appropriate
enough for *A Lost Lady,* where the principal character
is closely related to her environment and can be effectively seen through the eyes of a representative of that
environment; but in *My Mortal Enemy* the change
from adventurous generosity to bitter resentment is the
product of poisons working within the character, and
these we are never allowed to see. One might say that the
perspective of the story is wrong. Willa Cather at her
best sees characters against a background which helps
to set the emotional tone proper to the personality she
is exploring; her backgrounds are lyrical and musical
rather than the piece-by-piece illustration of the impact
of *this* aspect of environment on *that* aspect of character.
My Mortal Enemy requires a more detailed and searching method to be thoroughly convincing, more meticulous documentation, the ability to marshal a great
number of details patiently and relentlessly. Instead,
she tried to do it in a few broad strokes, and though
these strokes are individually skillful, and there are
several incidents in the novel which show real perception and a feeling for the specific situation, there is no
cumulative massing of effects to achieve the inevitable
end which this kind of story must have if it is not to appear altogether too arbitrary and *voulu. My Mortal
Enemy* is thus a parergon of considerable interest to
students of Miss Cather's art, illustrating its limitations,
and, negatively, pointing up her characteristic excel-
lences: but it is not in itself a wholly successful work.

We have seen the Southwest gradually ousting the Midwest in Willa Cather's novels. Claude, in *One of Ours,* is in revolt against the commercial values which the grandsons of the pioneers have imposed on farming life, and henceforth Miss Cather looks for her symbols of value elsewhere. The heroine of *A Lost Lady* is lost because western society can no longer provide her with an appropriately heroic environment. Professor St. Peter in *The Professor's House* has a kind of heroism which modern society neither recognizes nor appreciates—even his love of fine sherry is out of place in a prohibitionist era. The professor finds his compensation in identifying himself in a sense with Tom Outland for whom, as for the professor, the romance of history takes the place of contemporary heroism. Beauty, order, and heroic action—three ideals which haunted the professor, and which he was unable to find in modern life —are to be found in the old Catholic Southwest. In *Death Comes for the Archbishop,* published in 1927, Miss Cather pursued her ideals into the history of that region of America to write a novel based upon the lives of Bishop Lamy of Sante Fe and Father Machebeuf, his vicar general. This novel marks the second major shift in Miss Cather's art, though the shift is not unexpected or unprepared for. The first was when she abandoned the Jamesian refinements of *Alexander's Bridge* for the robust handling of her familiar Nebraska in *O Pioneers!* and subsequent novels. As the ideals represented by her midwestern novels disappear in modern life, she moves toward history, indirectly in *The Professor's House,* directly in *Death Comes for the*

Archbishop. Death Comes for the Archbishop is a historical novel; it is also a regional novel and a deliberately picturesque novel, with natural description helping to set the emotional tone as it did for *O Pioneers!* and *My Ántonia.* The ritual and beliefs of the Catholic Church, the heroic activity of missionary priests, and the vivid colors of the southwestern landscape combine to produce a new kind of warmth and vitality in her art.

Death Comes for the Archbishop is the best known and most popular of Miss Cather's novels, perhaps because its qualities, though considerable, are rather obvious. An episodic and sentimental novel which exploits a cultured religious heroism in a context of picturesque landscape and romantic historical figures, a novel both sophisticated and elemental, both meditative and full of action, an epic success story with a brightly colored surface—such a novel could hardly fail to be acclaimed as her most effective work to date. Yet one wonders whether this lively creation of a golden world in which all ideals are realized is not fundamentally a "softer" piece of writing than, say, *My Ántonia* with its frustrations counterbalancing successes, or than *The Professor's House,* whose main note is of heroic failure. There is, it is true, a splendid sympathy in the treatment of the characters and a most genuine feeling for the period and the natural setting in which the action is laid. But there is no indication here of an artist wrestling successfully with intractable material. The material is all too tractable, and the success, though it is real enough, seems too easy.

Yet it would be unfair to quarrel with a novel for being too obviously a success. Certainly, the ease and confidence of the writing are not qualities we should wish away. "Writing this book . . . ," wrote Willa Cather in a letter to *The Commonweal* in November, 1927, "was like a happy vacation from life, a return to childhood, to early memories." It has about it the air of a happy vacation, a relaxed air, in spite of the detail and the brightness.

In writing *Death Comes for the Archbishop* Miss Cather was drawing on her own memories of travel in the Southwest some fifteen years before the publication of the book. She spent a considerable time there, traveling slowly by wagon and carrying a camp outfit, and learned a great deal about the history and traditions of New Mexico from Father Haltermann, a Belgian priest at Santa Cruz.

The longer I stayed in the Southwest, the more I felt that the story of the Catholic Church in that country was the most interesting of all its stories. The old mission churches, even those which were abandoned and in ruins, had a moving reality about them; the hand-carved beams and joists, the utterly unconventional frescoes, the countless fanciful figures of the saints, no two of them alike, seemed a direct expression of some very real and lively human feeling. They were all fresh, individual, first-hand.

Miss Cather revisited New Mexico and Arizona many times after her first trip there, and became ever more interested in the story of the Church and the Spanish missionaries, especially Archbishop Lamy, the first Bishop of New Mexico. In 1925 she "came upon a book printed years ago on a country press at Pueblo, Colorado: *The Life of the Right Reverend Joseph P. Machebeuf,* by William Joseph Howlett, a priest who had worked with Father Machebeuf in Denver." This book, which included information acquired in France from Father Machebeuf's sister Philomène and letters from Father Machebeuf to his sister, gave her the kind of background she was looking for. Father Machebeuf is the Father Joseph Vaillant of the novel, friend and helper of the Bishop (whose name in the novel is Jean Marie Latour). "What I got from Father Machebeuf's letters," Miss Cather wrote, "was the mood, the spirit in which they accepted the accidents and hardships of a desert country, the joyful energy that kept them going. To attempt to convey this hardihood of spirit one must use language a little stiff, a little formal, one must not be afraid of the old trite phraseology of the frontier. Some of those time-worn phrases I used as the note from the piano by which the violinist tunes his instrument." The book took only a few months to write, because it "had all been lived many times before it was written, and the happy mood in which I began it never paled." [1]

Death Comes for the Archbishop opens with a prologue at Rome in 1848. "Three Cardinals and a missionary Bishop from America" are discussing the founding of an Apostolic Vicarate in New Mexico, a region recently annexed to the United States. The Bishop from America urges consideration of Jean Marie

[1] These quotations are from Miss Cather's letter to *The Commonweal,* which is reprinted in *Willa Cather on Writing.*

Latour for the new position. He is a Frenchman, at present a parish priest working on the shores of Lake Ontario, a man fitted by character and intelligence to undertake the arduous task of reviving a lively Catholic faith in a part of the world which had been evangelized by the Franciscan Fathers in 1500 but where now the old mission churches are in ruins, the few priests are lax and ignorant, and adequate religious instruction is unavailable to the people.

(In this prologue the contrast between the sophisticated cardinals at Rome, with their connoisseurship in art and wines, their intellectual finesse, and their tendency to see American affairs through European spectacles, on the one hand, and the arduous and exacting task that awaits the new Vicar Apostolic in New Mexico on the other, is effectively emphasized. As the story develops, these two sides are to be brought closer together, for religion, as Miss Cather now sees it, stands for the arts of life in every sense (a far cry indeed from the pallid religion of Enid in *One of Ours!*), and she has gone to contemporary New Mexico in order to find the kind of pattern in living that the professor was unable to find in contemporary Michigan.)

After the prologue, the novel proper begins with a formal, rather old-fashioned opening: "One afternoon in the autumn of 1851 a solitary horseman, followed by a pack-mule, was pushing through an arid stretch of country somewhere in central New Mexico."

The horseman is, of course, Latour, now Vicar Apostolic of New Mexico and Bishop of Agathonica *in partibus*. He is on his way through lonely and barren country to find the Bishop of Durango, under whose jurisdiction the priests of Santa Fe had formerly been, and to clarify his position. This opening incident illustrates the hardships, excitements, and rewards of the life he has now embarked on: he is lost but unexpectedly finds a hospitable village of "little adobe houses with brilliant gardens," a Mexican settlement where Catholic piety still lives on though no priest has been there for generations. Here he celebrates Mass, performs marriages and baptisms, hears confessions, confirms—activities that he and Father Vaillant are to perform in countless other forgotten settlements in the coming years—before proceeding on his way. Thus the picaresque note is sounded, and the episodic nature of the action suggested.

In her letter to *The Commonweal* Miss Cather remarked that she preferred to call this book a narrative rather than a novel. "But a novel, it seems to me, is merely a work of imagination in which a writer tries to present the experiences and emotions of a group of people by the light of his own. That is what he really does, whether his method is 'objective' or 'subjective.' " Miss Cather lets her imagination play about these two priests in their journeyings and ministrations, their endeavors to build on the old foundations a lively yet disciplined Catholic life against a background of Indian customs and superstitious Mexican fears and prejudices, and a brilliantly colorful landscape. The dying civilization of the Indians plays an effective part as a minor theme running through the novel, providing just a trace of an elegiac mood. But the dominant mood is far from elegiac: it is robust and adventurous, though softened at intervals by carefully placed flash backs dealing with the youth of her two heroes in France. By the end of the novel nostalgia for France has been sublimated into an intense affection for the new country which, insofar as they are making it more Catholic, they are Europeanizing. In the bright sunshine of New Mexico the mellower values of European civilization mingle with memories of New Spain, relics of the old Indian way of life, and the challange of the New World, to produce, at last, a combination of Old and New World values that thoroughly satisfied the author. We have seen Miss Cather facing this problem in earlier novels: now she finds in the civilization of the Catholic Southwest a symbolic solution.

Book Two, "Missionary Journeys," consists of two episodes, one concerning Father Vaillant and one in which both he and the Bishop are involved. The episodes are narrated with a lively shrewdness—a tone not previously discernible in Miss Cather's work. She seems to be trying to convey in the very quality of her writing something of the simple folk virtues of the Mexican characters she introduces, their combination of humor, cunning, indolence, and generosity. Father Vaillant with his warmth, energy, and genuine love of people, can meet them on their own ground with immense success; Father Latour meets them with dignity rather than familiarity and is successful in a different way, especially with the Indians. As the episodes follow each other the characters of the two priests emerge ever more strongly and clearly defined, the nature of their endeavor and the source of their inspiration become clearer, and always the background of old mission churches, simple piety and superstition, Mexican and Indian fears of the new American civilization of which they are now supposed to be a part, and the Catholic ritual of the Christian year weaves in and out of the narrative to provide its special richness and flavor.

In spite of vast journeyings, by the beginning of Book Three Bishop Latour has not yet begun to explore his great diocese:

> So far, Bishop Latour had been mainly employed on business that took him away from his Vicarate. His great diocese was still an unimaginable mystery to him. He was eager to be abroad in it, to know his people; to escape for a little from the cares of building and founding, and to go westward among the old isolated Indian missions; Santo Domingo, breeder of horses; Isleta, whitened with gypsum; Laguna, of wide pastures; and finally, cloud-set Ácoma.

He sets out "in the golden October weather" to visit the Indian missions in the west. These visits bring him into conflict with the old Mexican priests who, long isolated from European Catholicism, have developed their own blend of Christianity and local superstitions. There is something magnificent about these half-pagan priests, many of whom make no pretense of keeping their vows; for all their moral laxity their religion has a picturesqueness and liveliness which the Bishop cannot help admiring. In Book Three we meet Padre Gallegos, who, although ten years older than the Bishop, "would still dance the fandango five nights running, as if he could never have enough of it." He is a genial, poker-playing, whisky-drinking priest belonging to an important Mexican family, and his popularity is enormous. As Bishop Latour leaves Albuquerque he meditates on the gay padre:

Yet, he reflected, there was something very engaging about Gallegos as a man. As a priest, he was impossible; he was too self-satisfied and popular ever to change his ways, and he certainly could not change his face. He did not look quite like a professional gambler, but something smooth and twinkling in his countenance suggested an underhanded mode of life. There was but one course: to suspend the man from the exercise of all priestly functions, and bid the smaller native priests take warning.

His case is easier to handle than that of Padre Martinez of Taos, whom we meet in Book Five. Martinez had instigated the revolt of the Taos Indians five years before, when the American Governor and other white men were murdered. Yet he had escaped punishment himself and had indeed managed to make a large profit out of the whole affair. He was a man of tremendous strength and imperious will. "His broad high shoulders were like a bull buffalo's, his big head was set defiantly on a thick neck, and the full-cheeked, richly coloured, egg-shaped Spanish face—how vividly the Bishop remembered that face! . . . His mouth was the very assertion of violent, uncurbed passions and tyrannical self-will; the full lips thrust out and taut, like the flesh of animals distended by fear or desire." Father Latour's visit to Padre Martinez and its aftermath is, like so many of the incidents in this novel, a complete short story in itself, done with great vividness. The sense of the picturesque, which is evident in Miss Cather's treatment of all these incidents, provides a kind of color and charm quite different from anything in *O Pioneers!* or *My Ántonia*.

It might almost be said that the moral pattern in *Death Comes for the Archbishop* is deficient because the author is warmly sympathetic to everybody. Except for one degenerate murderer, who figures in the second of the two episodes in Book Two, there is hardly a character in the whole novel who is not admirable in his way, and since Father Latour looks at the characters with the same understanding eyes as Miss Cather herself, there is a certain failure to project with complete conviction the significance of his missionary impulse. The qualities which Miss Cather admired in New Mexican life were, indeed, the qualities to be found there before her two heroes came on the scene. The baptizings, confirmings, marryings, and similar activities carried on by Father Latour and Father Vaillant appear more as efforts to tidy things up or as excuses for fascinating journeys than as the manifestations of a significant new religious life. Only toward the end of the book, when Father Vaillant goes off to the Colorado Rockies to work heroically among the lawless society of gold seekers, does it appear that really significant religious change is to result. The Bishop, for all his strenuous endeavors, grows into his new environment rather than changes it, and when the book has come to an end we have the impression of a life devoted to the thoughtful and sympathetic merging of a French Catholic youth into a New Mexican middle and old age. When death comes for the Archbishop, he returns to die in Santa Fe, in which the only change for the better since his first arrival is "the golden face of his Cathedral": returning to his beloved Santa Fe, he dies thinking of his youth in France. His greatest achievement has been to merge the two happily in his consciousness.

Book Four is devoted to an incident illustrating the Indian background of New Mexican life, and here, as usual, the incidents are narrated with warmth and vividness. Book Five belongs to Pedro Martinez, and Book Six tells with great verve a rather obviously picturesque story of the widow of a rich Mexican *ranchero* who must tell in court the bitter truth about her real age if she is to prove her right to her husband's bequest. Book Six concentrates on the relations between the Bishop and Father Vaillant, a slow-moving and sincerely imagined exploration of the love between two very different but mutually devoted priests and the relation of that love to their religious ambitions. It also includes the incident, "December Night," which has been printed separately as a short story—the story of an ill-treated slave finding her way to the church one night a few weeks before Christmas and there meeting the Bishop, who blesses and comforts her. It is a story whose emotional overtones are rather obvious: it has the tone and the coloring of a Christmas card.

Book Eight tells of the Bishop's ambition to build a cathedral out of the yellow rock he found in a ridge high

above the Rio Grande valley and closes with news of
the appalling situation in the camps under Pike's Peak,
where the Colorado gold rush had drawn thousands of
people to live "adrift in a lawless society without spirit-
ual guidance." Father Vaillant, who has been recalled
from Albuquerque by the Bishop to afford himself some
congenial company, sets out on his final and most arduous round of missionary activity. In Colorado, we are
told briefly later, he rises to new heights of adventurous
priestly functioning, to die there at last amid universal
mourning.

In Book Nine, which concludes the novel, the Bishop
has become an Archbishop and has retired to a small
country estate. We are given a careful account of his
state of mind during the days that immediately precede
his death, and the book ends quietly. The title, it should
be noted (which comes from Holbein's *Dance of Death*),
is quite misleading. The Archbishop's death is a brief
episode, rounding out a full life, and it is the full life
which is the subject of the novel. Latour is not even an
archbishop until the last few pages of the book. Willa
Cather, as has been more than once observed, was
singularly inept at choosing titles. *Death Comes for the
Archbishop* is a title which suggests a novel centered on
the last year's of the hero's life, a meditative novel in
which, as he lies dying, he looks back on and sums up
the meaning of his life's work; or something like Victoria Sackville-West's *All Passion Spent*. Perhaps the
most baffling of all Miss Cather's titles is *One of Ours*;
but *The Song of the Lark*, as she recognized in the introduction to the 1937 edition, is also a confusing and mis-

leading title, and even *O Pioneers!* (from Whitman) does not suggest the kind of novel which the book actually is.

But the book is more important than its title and more interesting than any summary of its incidents may suggest. Some of the minor themes which weave in and out are treated with great skill. Gardening is one of these themes: the two priests, like their Spanish and Mexican predecessors, were always concerned with making that thirsty land as fruitful as possible, and discussions of flowers and vegetables, anecdotes illustrating how fruit trees came to be planted and nurtured, how European palates produced a modification of native growths and habits, run cheerfully through the book. Even the legend of Fray Baltazar, the early eighteenth-century priest who devoted too much time to good living and cultivated a wonderful fruit and vegetable garden at Ácoma only to come to a sticky end when his zeal as a *bon viveur* overcame his discretion as a man and a priest, has a gay abandon about it.

Weaving through the American adventures of the two priests are also recollections of their childhood and youth in Auvergne; these recollections are presented with a subdued lyrical nostalgia which, as the book progresses, is carried over to their first American experiences. Miss Cather has made effective use of the letters from Machebeuf to his sister Philomène which Father Howlett inserted in his life of Machebeuf. Yet the texture of the book remains surprisingly even: for all the variety of incident and anecdote the dominant mood—a mood of sunny determination flowering out of deep sensibility—is never allowed to vanish for long. Stories of miracles and of acts of simple piety by humble folk combine with the description of natural scenery to present the background of primitive and elemental beauty against which the subtler sensibility of the Bishop is set and with which it achieves harmony.

It is not easy to illustrate the quality of *Death Comes for the Archbishop* by quotation, for the effect is achieved cumulatively; but the following paragraphs illustrate something of the combination of matter-of-fact narrative with warm and rich overtones, the combination of new observation with old recollection, the use of detail and of color, which are to be found in a style which remains nevertheless surprisingly simple:

Father Vaillant had told the Bishop that he must by all means stop a night at Isleta, as he would like the priest there —Padre Jesus de Baca, an old white-haired man, almost blind, who had been at Isleta many years and had won the confidence and affection of his Indians.

When he approached this pueblo of Isleta, gleaming white across a low plain of grey sand, Father Latour's spirits rose. It was beautiful, that warm, rich whiteness of the church and the clustered town, shaded by a few bright acacia trees, with their intense blue-green like the colour of old paper window-blinds. That tree always awakened pleasant memories, recalling a garden in the south of France where he used to visit young cousins. As he rode up to the church, the old priest came out to meet him, and after his salutation stood looking at Father Latour, shading his failing eyes with his hand.

"And can this be my Bishop? So young a man?" he exclaimed.

They went into the priest's house by way of a garden, walled in behind the church. This enclosure was full of domesticated cactus plants, of many varieties and great size (it seemed the Padre loved them), and among these hung wicker cages made of willow twigs, full of parrots. There were even parrots hopping about the sanded paths,—with one wing clipped to keep them at home. Father Jesus explained that parrot feathers were much prized by his Indians as ornaments for their ceremonial robes, and he had long ago found he could please his parishioners by raising the birds.

The priest's house was white within and without, like all the Isleta houses, and was almost as bare as an Indian dwelling. The old man was poor, and too soft-hearted to press the pueblo people for pesos. An Indian girl cooked his beans and cornmeal mush for him, he required little else. The girl was not very skilful, he said, but she was clean about her cooking. When the Bishop remarked that everything in this pueblo, even the streets, seemed clean, the Padre told him that near Isleta there was a hill of some white mineral, which the Indians ground up and used as whitewash. They had done this from time immemorial, and the village had always been noted for its whiteness. A little talk with Father Jesus revealed that he was simple almost to childishness, and very superstitious. But there was a quality of golden goodness about him. His right eye was overgrown by a cataract, and he kept his head tilted as if he were trying to see around it. All his movements were to the left, as if he were reaching or walking about some obstacle in his path.

This is a "soft" style perhaps; it has a self-conscious primitivism about it; but it does succeed admirably in achieving the effects its author intended.

The Claims of History

Shadows on the Rock, published in 1931, does for Quebec in the late seventeenth and early eighteenth century what *Death Comes for the Archbishop* had done for nineteenth-century New Mexico. Here again Willa Cather found a historical situation in which the impact of the Old World on the New produced a result which seemed to her culturally satisfying. The story—or rather, the series of incidents, for the novel is even more episodic in structure than *Death Comes for the Archbishop*—is set on the rock of Quebec and explores the quality of the French civilization which had developed there. The title is here more appropriate than in most of her novels. "I tried, as you say," she wrote to Governor Wilbur Cross, acknowledging his appreciative review of the book, "to state the mood and the viewpoint in the title. To me the rock of Quebec is not only a stronghold on which many strange figures have for a little time cast a shadow in the sun; it is the curious endurance of a kind of culture, narrow but definite." She was deliberately trying to discover and express a kind of culture very different from the pioneering culture of the West which she had explored in her early novels, yet equally different from the sunny primitivism of the Southwest:

There, among the country people and the nuns, I caught something new to me; a kind of feeling about life and human fate that I could not accept, wholly, but which I could not but admire. It is hard to state that feeling in language; it was more like an old song, incomplete but uncorrupted, than like a legend. . . . I took the incomplete air and tried to give it what would correspond to a sympathetic musical setting; tried to develop it into a prose composition not too conclusive, not too definite: a series of pictures remembered rather than experienced; a kind of thinking, a mental complexion inherited, left over from the past, lacking in robustness and full of pious resignation.

Now, it seemed to me that the mood of the misfits among the early settlers (and there were a good many) must have been just that. An orderly little French household that went on trying to live decently, just as ants begin to rebuild when you kick their house down, interests me more than Indian raids or the wild life in the forests.[2]

The story is centered on the widowed apothecary Euclide Auclair, who had come to Canada from Paris with his patron the Count de Frontenac and his thirteen-year-old daughter Cécile. The domestic setting of the apothecary's house in the shadow of château, convent, and cathedral sets the tone for the novel. "On a heavy morning, when clouds of thick grey fog rolled up from the St. Lawrence, it cheered one to go into a place that was like an apothecary's shop at home; to glimpse the comfortable sitting-room through the tall cabinets and chests of drawers that separated without entirely shutting it off from the shop." The practices and ritual of the Catholic church are closely associated with this domestic atmosphere, while the plans of European statesmen and ecclesiastics, which set this whole new civilization going in the first place, loom in the distant background. Once having settled on the domestic tone, "once having taken your seat in the close air by the

[2] Miss Cather's letter to Wilbur Cross was published in *The Saturday Review of Literature* (October 17, 1931) and reprinted in *Willa Cather on Writing*.

apothecary's fire, you can't explode into military glory, any more than you can pour champagne into a salad dressing. . . . And really, a new society begins with the salad dressing more than with the destruction of Indian villages. Those people brought a kind of French culture there and somehow kept it alive on that rock, sheltered it and tended it and on occasion died for it, as if it really were a sacred fire—and all this temperately and shrewdly, with emotion always tempered by good sense."

Perhaps more explicitly than in any other of her novels, Miss Cather here explores the transplantation of a culture. Again and again in the course of the novel she lays her pen down, as it were, to speculate about this theme. "When an adventurer carries his gods with him into a remote and savage country," she remarks in the middle of Book Two, "the colony he founds will, from the beginning, have graces, traditions, riches of the mind and spirit. Its history will shine with bright incidents, slight, perhaps, but precious, as in life itself, where the great matters are often as worthless as astronomical distances, and the trifles dear as the heart's blood."

As the narrative develops, appropriate flash backs fill in the details of the apothecary's earlier life, of the history and character of the rugged old Bishop Laval and his willful and unpopular successor, and of the life of Count Frontenac, the old soldier who served his country nobly but had met with indifference and ingratitude from King Louis and died at last in virtual exile at Quebec. These flash backs enlarge in some degree the scope of the novel and give us some awareness of the relation of the foreground to the background, but the emphasis throughout is on the foreground, on the daily life of these early inhabitants of "Kebec." The spotlight remains for the most part on Cécile, a true Canadian, who grew up on the rock of Quebec and regards it, with the countryside around it, as the only place where she can ever really be at home. Her father's mind harks back continually to Paris, while Cécile belongs to Canada: the apothecary is described as making for himself in Quebec as close a replica of his Paris life as he can —this, too, had been the main objective of his wife on her arrival; but Cécile, while she appreciates and enjoys the solid bourgeois comforts of her father's house and is disgusted with the dirt and coarseness she finds when she pays a visit to a more primitive settlement, thinks of what the French have built in Quebec as typically Canadian and can never dissociate it from the river and the woods, the colorful autumns and the brilliant, cold winters, of the only world she really knows. The resolution of such rudimentary plot as the novel contains is achieved when Cécile learns that the Count has not been recalled to France as he expected to be and that therefore her father will remain with his patron in Canada. All during the fall she had been upset by her father's preparations for their return—preparations symbolized by his taking down his herbarium from its accustomed shelf, before deciding which native herbs he would take back with him to Paris. But now that he is not returning to Paris, peace descends again on the household:

The Claims of History

No more boats to France would come to Quebec as late as this, even her father admitted that, and his herbarium had been put back on the high shelves of the cabinet, where it belonged. As soon as those dried plants were out of sight, the house itself changed; everything seemed to draw closer together, to join hands, as it were. Cécile had polished the candlesticks and pewter cups, rubbed the table and the bedposts and the chair-claws with oil, darned the rent in her father's counterpane. A little more colour had come back into the carpet and the curtains, she thought. Perhaps that was only because the fire was lit in the salon every evening now, and things always looked better in the fire-light. But no, she really believed that everything in the house, the furniture, the china shepherd boy, the casseroles in the kitchen, knew that the herbarium had been restored to the high shelves and that the world was not going to be destroyed this winter.

This feeling of drawing the curtains on a cosy interior emerges again in the final paragraph of the epilogue, which is set fifteen years after the main action. Cécile is married now, and the unpopular young Bishop has returned to Quebec, after a long absence, an old and chastened man, to tell news of changes and threatened dangers in the French political scene. But the expected death of Louis XIV with the difficulties it would bring in its wake seem very far away from these French Canadians. The apothecary, having listened to the Bishop tell of these things, finally gives up his thoughts of France and, as his daughter had done earlier, thinks with satisfaction of Canada's isolation from Europe:

While he was closing his shop and changing his coat to
go up to his daughter's house, he thought over much that
his visitor had told him, and he believed that he was indeed
fortunate to spend his old age here where nothing changed;
to watch his grandsons grow up in a country where the death
of the King, the probable evils of a long regency, would
never touch them.

Yet Canada is not in any real sense opposed to France,
or to the Old World in general, as a new civilization.
Quebec is what it is precisely because it *is* France—
transplanted. But it is France transplanted in a new soil,
and the new growth thus naturally differs from the old.
The new environment—the changing seasons as they
affect living both outdoors and indoors, the background
of adventure and exploration, the tenuous contact with
the Old World symbolized by the annual arrival of ships
from France each summer—is studied with care and
presented in vivid and picturesque prose. The novel
opens with the departure of the ships for France late in
October, 1697, thus cutting Quebec off from all contact
with Europe until the following summer. Having thus
drawn the curtains on the colony, Miss Cather proceeds
to explore its natural scenery and its domestic interiors.

The Château Saint-Louis, grey stone with steep dormer
roofs, on the very edge of the cliff overlooking the river, sat
level; but just beside it the convent and church of the Récol-
let friars ran downhill, as if it were sliding backwards. To
landward, in a low, well-sheltered spot, lay the Convent of
the Ursulines . . . lower still stood the massive foundation
of the Jesuits, facing the Cathedral. Immediately behind the
Cathedral the cliff ran up sheer again. . . .

The Claims of History

Not one building on the rock was on the same level with any other,—and two hundred feet below them all was the Lower Town, crowded along the narrow strip of beach between the river's edge and the perpendicular face of the cliff. The Lower Town was so directly underneath the Upper Town that one could stand on the terrace of the Château Saint-Louis and throw a stone down into the narrow streets below.

These heavy grey buildings, monasteries and churches, steep-pitched and dormered, with spires and slated roofs, were roughly Norman Gothic in effect. They were made by people from the north of France who knew no other way of building. The settlement looked like something cut off from one of the ruder towns of Normandy or Brittany, and brought over. It was indeed a rude beginning of a "new France," of a Saint-Malo or Rouen or Dieppe, anchored here in the ever-changing northern light and weather. . . .

On the opposite shore of the river, just across from the proud rock of Quebec, the black pine forest came down to the water's edge; and on the west, behind the town, the forest stretched no living man knew how far. That was the dead, sealed world of the vegetable kingdom, an uncharted continent choked with interlocking trees, living, dead, half-dead, their roots in bogs and swamps, strangling each other in a slow agony that had lasted for centuries. The forest was suffocation, annihilation; there European man was quickly swallowed up in silence, distance, mould, black mud, and the stinging swarms of insect life that bred in it. The only avenue of escape was along the river. The river was the one thing that lived, moved, glittered, changed,—a highway along which men could travel, taste the sun and open air, feel freedom, join their fellows, reach the open sea . . . reach the world, even!

Willa Cather

Around this settlement the ecclesiastical atmosphere is heavy. Miss Cather was as fascinated with Catholicism in Quebec as she had been with the Catholic civilization of the Southwest. Cécile, with her love of stories about saints and martyrs, keeps the reader continually aware of the Catholic milieu in which all these people move; while glimpses of old Bishop Laval, stories of dedicated nuns and heroic missionary priests, and religious anecdotes of all kinds, emphasize that the culture of New France is far from secular. In *Death Comes for the Archbishop*, where the two principal characters are priests and the book is chiefly concerned with ecclesiastical and religious matters, this religious anecdotalism (if one might call it so in no spirit of disrespect) is perfectly appropriate; but in *Shadows on the Rock* one has the feeling that it is overdone. In her zeal to do full justice to the Catholic element in the life of Kebec, Miss Cather packs in so many references to and stories about religious activities of one kind and another that the reader —at least the lay reader—becomes impatient with the clerical atmosphere and wishes for at least one episode that is free from it. This is not to question the historical accuracy of Miss Cather's picture but to doubt the aesthetic appropriateness of so much detail of this kind.

The individual characters are clearly, but not sharply, drawn; their personalities are vivid and often highly colored. The dutiful and affectionate Cécile; her calm and thoughtful father; the gentle and sensitive little Jacques (son of a worthless mother and an absconded father); the sturdy and kindly fur trader Pierre Charron, whom Cécile eventually marries; the noble but disillusioned old Count; the rugged but saintly Bishop Laval and his flamboyant and stiff-necked successor—these are all deliberate portraits in a gallery of early Quebec types, and each has his character illustrated by appropriate anecdotes; but for all their individuality they lack the finer touches of portrait painting. They belong rather too obviously to a historical novel.

As a historical novel, *Shadows on the Rock* has an impressive surface brilliance. It is in its way a highly finished performance, with its careful fitting of character to environment, its deep sense of the needs and achievements, the nostalgia and the adjustments, the mingling of old and new loyalties, of the early settlers. Particularly effective is the use made of domestic interiors and the way in which they are related, in ever-widening circles, to the settlement on the rock as a whole, to the challenging world of nature beyond, and to the Old World across the ocean. (As in *Death Comes for the Archbishop,* an elegiac note of Old World scenes and memories sounds in the background) but the sound is fainter in this novel, and the emphasis is more firmly on what the New World has to offer. Its heroine is Cécile, who belongs wholeheartedly to Canada, and she marries a Canadian fur trader who thinks with nothing but distaste of the customs and restrictions which would limit his activities as hunter and seeker of adventure if he lived in old France. Yet even Cécile is the product of a French culture deliberately cultivated in a new environment. The relation between the two worlds remains after all fluid and indefinable, as it was to be two centuries later when the Shimerdas came to Nebraska. The problem of the French in Quebec was, however, much simpler than that of the Shimerdas in Nebraska, for the French were a homogeneous group deliberately transplanting a single culture while the Shimerdas were faced with a very different kind of assimilation. In the later novels Miss Cather deals with simpler situations— situations, moreover, that were simplified in historical retrospect. They gain in smoothness and finish, in all the more obvious aspects of craftsmanship; but the student of Miss Cather's career as a novelist cannot help wondering sometimes whether there is not an equivalent loss—a loss not easy to define, and perhaps not a loss in literary terms at all, but rather a lowering of the passion and vitality in the character of the writer that is discernible behind her work.

CHAPTER 5

The Novel Démeublé

WILLA CATHER's last two novels, *Lucy Gayheart* (1935) and *Sapphira and the Slave Girl* (1940), are hardly what one would have expected as the final work of an author who had moved from a self-conscious Jamesian craftsmanship through an exploration of the impact of the Old World on the New in the American Middle West, in which she drew on her autobiography, to a symbolization in historical novels of satisfying cultural patterns which she could not find in contemporary American civilization. *Lucy Gayheart* is the story, set in 1902, of a lively and attractive young girl in a Nebraskan small town who goes to Chicago to study music and falls in love with a middle-aged singer for whom she is acting as temporary accompanist; her love for him leads her to refuse somewhat roughly the offer of marriage made to her by her native town's wealthiest and most charming young man; but the brief idyll which she and the singer share is shattered when the singer, having gone back to Europe for the summer, is drowned in a boating accident on Lake Como. The heroine, returning home from Chicago numbed and wretched, meets her death shortly afterward, also by drowning, in a skating accident. An epilogue, set in 1927, gives the reactions and subsequent histories of the people in her native town who were most closely associated with her. *Sapphira and the Slave Girl* is set in Virginia just before the Civil War and tells how a beautiful slave girl produces an estrangement between a husband and his suspicious, invalid wife and brings on herself such persecution by the wife that she finally escapes to Canada and freedom. Here, too, there is an epilogue, set twenty-five years later, in which we are shown the eventual successful establishment in life of the former slave and in which the surviving characters get together for sentimental reminiscence.

Such themes hardly sound like Willa Cather. There are, it is true, echoes of *The Song of the Lark* in *Lucy Gayheart,* though the emphasis is quite different. The scenes of Chicago musical life, which are done with such richness and passion in *The Song of the Lark,* have a rather faded quality in the later novel. There is none of that vibrant quality at the heart of the work that we find in *The Song of the Lark,* and for all the deftness of the writing and the skill with which she occasionally projects the symbolic incident, *Lucy Gayheart* is in many ways more conventional in tone and quality than any novel Miss Cather had yet written. She appears to be rehandling old material without any compelling need to do so, with the result that the emotional pattern, so important an element in the earlier novels and indeed the element out of which everything else grows, is here hardly discernible. The gay Lucy and her somber middle-aged lover move about in the Chicago of 1902 in a series of gestures which are ably enough presented but are not realized with that power and urgency that make the presentation of Thea Kronborg's early years so memorable. And in the latter part of the novel, when rich young Harry Gordon has, in a fit of pique, married somebody else and snubs the dazed Lucy in order to prevent himself from revealing that he still loves her, the virtuosity of the writing seems to lack a proper object. The manipulation of Lucy into the ice, so that she may follow her drowned lover, is too obviously contrived, and the final picture of the survivors twenty-five years later ties up ends and underlines meanings with an excessive deliberation.

The other characters—Lucy's elder sister Pauline, who keeps house for her widowed father while Lucy goes off to Chicago to pursue her musical studies; the father, a cheerful and somewhat shiftless watchmaker and flute player who conducts the town band; Jimmy Mockford, the lame accompanist, with his strange, jealous attitude to the singer and to Lucy; Giuseppe, the Italian valet; Fairy Blair, the vulgar little flirt; wise old Mrs. Ramsay; Milton Chase, the bank clerk—are done with skill and a feeling for what might be called the atmosphere of personality, but they are all deliberate studies in character rather than persons who take their place naturally and inevitably in the development of the story. *Lucy Gayheart* is certainly the work of an accomplished and experienced writer, and we read it with interest and pleasure—but not with real conviction, and not with the excitement that a novel by Willa Cather in the fullness of her powers might be expected to produce.

Willa Cather

One remembers individual scenes rather than the shape of the novel as a whole, particularly the early scenes between Lucy and the singer, Clement Sebastian. If there is a touch of Hollywood about some of them, it can be maintained that it is good Hollywood, and good Hollywood has its place in this kind of literature. The conclusion, where Harry Gordon, now a man of over fifty, meditates over the footsteps in the concrete that Lucy had made some thirty-five years before, is sentimental but not wildly or inappropriately so. This is a sentimental story and has a faded charm appropriate to its kind.

A strong inventive imagination was not one of Willa Cather's gifts. Her memory had to be stirred, her emotions involved, some autobiographical impulse had to be touched, however indirectly, before she could produce her best and strongest work. And her best work *is* strong: she possessed the kind of masculine sensibility which drew nourishment from simple, elemental situations to subtilize them and make them persuasive symbols of aspects of experience much more complex than the narrative line of the story or the straightforwardness of the prose style might in themselves suggest. That strength is absent in *Lucy Gayheart,* a feminine and sentimental novel, which has both perceptiveness and stylistic grace yet lacks the characteristic Cather vitality. In retreating from the earthy situations of her earlier Midwestern novels she had finally lost altogether the epic touch, and, though she had gained other qualities, none of them were so convincingly her own. We have noticed the loss of vitality in *Death Comes for the*

Archbishop and *Shadows on the Rock* compared with some of the earlier novels, but in *Death Comes for the Archbishop* and *Shadows on the Rock* this loss is in some degree compensated for by picturesqueness and sharp colors, and most of all by an outgoing sympathy that flows from the author toward her characters.

Sapphira and the Slave Girl is set in the country of Willa Cather's own early childhood and utilizes surnames familiar to her from the conversation of her father and mother; but there is no autobiographical impulse here of the kind that helped to set the emotional tone for *O Pioneers!* and *My Antonia*. There are some echoes of earlier themes. Sapphira Colbert has something in her both of the lost lady and of the heroine of *My Mortal Enemy*. Her husband, Henry Colbert, the miller, has some touches of the miller in *One of Ours*. Martin Colbert, Henry's swaggering nephew, is Willa Cather's final picture of the rake, a character she had toyed with but not seriously presented in earlier novels. The book as a whole, however, is quite different in tone and emphasis from anything she had yet written.

The novel has two main centers of interest. One is the relationship between Henry and Sapphira, in some ways an oddly assorted couple, for Sapphira was the daughter of a wealthy and aristocratic Pennsylvania family of English descent and Henry came of a humble family of Flemish millers. On marrying Henry (to everybody's surprise) Sapphira moved away from her native county and settled on some property she owned in Back Creek, Virginia, where her husband became the local miller. Tensions between husband and wife arise in part from their different social backgrounds and from the different value standards which result. They are increased by the background of conflicting views regarding slavery, for in this part of the country northern attitudes were as common as southern, and nobody was very comfortable about the situation. And this brings us to the novel's second main center of interest, the position of the slave girl Nancy, devoted to the miller and anxious to serve him, and regarded by him in turn with an affectionate benevolence. The gossip of a jealous slave arouses Sapphira's suspicions (which have no foundation in fact) that Nancy and her husband are more intimately associated than as master and servant. Since Sapphira suffers from dropsy and is unable to walk, and her husband spends his nights alone down at the mill, she is all the readier to lend an ear to malicious gossip. Nancy, who has hitherto been her favorite, is now subjected by her to a series of petty persecutions which culminate in her inviting her husband's rakish nephew Martin to stay with them for the express (though of course unacknowledged) purpose of seducing Nancy and thus putting an end to her supposed affair with the miller. Martin loses no time in making his attempts on Nancy; he makes her life so miserable that she is driven in desperation to seek assistance from friends who put her in touch with the underground railroad to Canada, where she succeeds in escaping.

Sapphira and the Slave Girl in some degree illustrates the position of slaves in Virginia just before the Civil War, yet it does so only indirectly and sporadically, and the book can in no sense be called a historical novel. The

ambiguous relation between Sapphira and her husband
is explored with some subtlety to the point of their rec-
onciliation after the death of a grandchild, and this
theme remains in the mind more clearly and impres-
sively than the story of Nancy, who is not drawn in any
great detail and whose function in developing tensions
between husband and wife is more that of a catalyst than
of active agent in her own right. Nancy remains a
passive figure throughout the body of the story, and
only in the final retrospect, when she reappears to tell
what has happened to her after she left Virginia, does
she emerge as someone who acts rather than as someone
acted upon; and this final reminiscence is so brief, being
little more than an epilogue or pendent to the main
story, that it cannot change her position in the novel as
a whole.

A minor theme is associated with Mrs. Blake, the
Colberts' widowed daughter, who, after a brilliant and
happy period with her husband in Washington, returned with her two young daughters to live in Back
Creek following the sudden death from yellow fever of
her husband and only son. Quite different from her
vivid and strong-willed mother, she now leads a life of
quiet charity, acting as nurse and comforter to the poor
and sick of the district. It is she who arranges for Nancy's
escape. The subdued, minor theme of Rachel Blake's
life weaves sadly through the story, giving an elegiac
air to the whole novel. This settlement of frustrated and
in some cases bewildered people in the backwoods of
Virginia seems out of the mainstream of all worth-while
life, and a strange note of sadness emerges from the story

as it proceeds. This part of Virginia seems somehow to be lost between two civilizations. The final paragraph of the book is a summing up by Till, the old servant, of Sapphira's life in Back Creek. Sapphira is now dead, and in the final reminiscent talk the whole story is gently pushed into the past: " 'She oughtn't never to a' come out here,' Till often said to me. 'She wasn't raised that way. Mrs. Matchem, down at the old place, never got over it that Miss Sapphy didn't buy in Chestnut Hill an' live like a lady, 'stead a' leavin' it to run down under the Bushwells, an' herself comin' out here where nobody was anybody much.' "

The introduction, in this final reminiscent section, of the narrator who tells the last scene as a youngster remembering the conversation of her elders, emphasizes the elegiac note and the feeling that all this belongs to the irrevocable past. So, in *Lucy Gayheart,* the death of old Mr. Gayheart, twenty-five years after his daughter's drowning, is recorded sadly as the end of a chapter:

It was sad, too, to see the last member of a family go out; to see a chapter closed, and a once familiar name on the way to be forgotten. There they were, the Gayhearts, in that little square of ground, the new grave standing open. Mr. Gayheart would lie between his long-dead wife and his daughter Lucy; the young people could not remember her at all. Pauline they remembered; she lay on Lucy's left. There were two little mounds in the lot; sons who died in childhood, it was said. And now the story was finished: no grandchildren, complete oblivion.

Neither *Death Comes for the Archbishop* nor *Shadows on the Rock,* both in their way historical novels, ends on such a note; they end on a note of achievement and promise, a note sounded even more strongly in *O Pioneers!* and *The Song of the Lark.* The conclusion of *The Song of the Lark*—"So, into all the little settlements of quiet people, tidings of what their boys and girls are doing in the world bring refreshment; bring to the old, memories, and to the young, dreams"—neatly relates the memories of the old to the dreams of the young to preserve the texture of a living civilization. Increasingly unable to find that texture in the present, the author records her sense of loss in such novels as *One of Ours* and *A Lost Lady* before going to seek it in the picturesque past. But in *Sapphira and the Slave Girl* the past is no longer picturesque—only confused, pathetic, and very far away.

Throughout the whole of the latter part of her career as a novelist Willa Cather kept protesting against the demands of naturalism in fiction; the selection of a few, properly symbolic objects, is what is needed, she claimed, rather than the minute and exact cataloging of as much as possible. In her essay, "The Novel Démeublé" ("unfurnished"), written in 1922, she quoted with approval Mérimée on Gogol: "L'art de choisir parmi les innombrables traits que nous offre la nature est, après tout, bien plus difficile que celui de les observer avec attention et de les rendre avec exactitude." ("The art of choosing among the innumerable strokes which nature offers us is, after all, much more difficult than that of observing them with attention and describing them with exactitude.") Fourteen years later, in a letter to *The Commonweal,* she attacked the notion of "social realism" so common in the thirties. In this letter she refused to consider "escapism" a bad word. "What has art ever been but escape?" The documentation of social evils for propaganda purposes has nothing, she claimed, to do with the artist as artist. "Anyone who looks over a collection of prehistoric Indian pottery dug up from old burial-mounds knows at once that the potters experimented with form and colour to gratify something that had no concern with food and shelter. The major arts (poetry, painting, architecture, sculpture, music) have a pedigree all their own. They did not come into being as a means of increasing the game supply or promoting tribal security. They sprang from an unaccountable predilection of the one unaccountable thing in man." [1]

This desire for unfurnishing the novel, combined with her repudiation of any obvious social function in fiction, might have led Miss Cather to a kind of subtle symbolic writing which woman novelists in England have in our time practiced so successfully. But, while in *The Professor's House* she comes as close as she ever did to this kind of writing, she did not take the path chosen by, say, Virginia Woolf. The influence of James is clear in *Alexander's Bridge,* but it never reappears in any obvious way. The influence of Proust is nowhere discernible. Yet James and Proust have been the novelists most influential on other twentieth-century writers who, like Willa Cather, have endeavored to "interpret imagina-

[1] "Escapism," reprinted in *Willa Cather on Writing,* where "The Novel Démeublé" is also reprinted.

tively [rather than naturally] the material and social investiture of their characters; to present their scene by suggestion rather than by enumeration." James and Proust are paramount, for example, in the heredity of Elizabeth Bowen's art. Willa Cather, however, was not interested in any kind of radical experimentation with the technique of the novel, and some interest of that kind was necessary to achieve the delicate texture of such a novel as *To the Lighthouse* or *The Death of the Heart*. Miss Cather's technique remained for the most part sturdily traditional. The opening of Book One of *Death Comes for the Archbishop* ("One afternoon in the autumn of 1851 a solitary horseman . . .") might have come—except for the date—from Scott or Fenimore Cooper or any one of a dozen minor historical novelists of the nineteenth century. It belongs to the "Two-travellers-might-have-been-seen" school of writing.

In her letter on escapism Miss Cather associated the demand for propagandist realism on the part of radicals with radicalism in literary *form,* thus using the term "literary radicals" very ambiguously. "So far, the effort to make a new kind of poetry, 'pure poetry,' which eschews (or renounces) the old themes as shop-worn, and confines itself to regarding the grey of a wet oyster shell against the sand of a wet beach through a drizzle of rain, has not produced anything very memorable," she remarks caustically; and it is curious to find this willful over-simplification of the issue by a distinguished novelist in 1936.

One wonders sometimes whether this belief in the

well-selected symbolic detail, combined with her suspicion of "radicalism" in technique does not explain the
qualities of her final novels. The symbolic qualities of
the novels of the Midwest are easy to see; the strokes
there are bold and lively. In subsequent novels picturesqueness compensates in some degree for boldness,
and in *Death Comes for the Archbishop,* for example,
history and geography combine to increase the symbolic
value of the detail. But where neither the history nor
the geography is exciting, and where the sense of personal implication is lacking, a certain lack of vitality is
bound to result in a novel that has been deliberately
démeublé. In fact, the novel démeublé, if it lacks these
other sources of vitality, requires a subtle lyrical style,
something less solid and opaque than the prose of the
traditional novel, if it is to be wholly successful. Willa
Cather could have learned from the so-called "stream-
of-consciousness" technique, and from many other ex-
perimental devices introduced in the early years of this
century, to give a new force to that somewhat chastened
vision which at the end she brought to bear on life.

CHAPTER 6

The Short Stories

IT WAS as a writer of short stories that Willa Cather made her first public literary appearance, and she continued to practice this form throughout her career. We have already noticed her undergraduate stories and mentioned her first collection, *The Troll Garden.* In spite of her own later dissatisfaction with three of the seven stories in *The Troll Garden,* the rejected stories are not greatly below those in *Youth and the Bright Medusa* in interest or craftsmanship, though they do possess a greater degree of stiffness in the dialogue.

The opening story, "Flavia and her Artists," is a rather too obviously contrived study of a woman who "collects" artists and considers herself more discerning in these matters than her devoted and generous husband, who accidentally discovers the true feeling which the collected artists have for his wife—one of contempt —and, while understanding the hysterical unreality of his wife's artistic enthusiasms, protects her from ever knowing the artists' real attitude to her at the expense of stigmatizing himself in her eyes as an unperceptive Philistine. The story is full of overt ironies, but the events are skillfully deployed and their presentation through the eyes of a thoughtful girl who is herself half in love with the lady's husband adds a touch of piquancy and considerable dramatic interest. "Flavia and her Artists" is stiff but well manipulated.

The other two of the subsequently rejected stories also deal with art and artists, though quite differently. "The Garden Lodge" tells of a girl whose father's shiftless romanticism kept his family in weary poverty, so that when she grew up and escaped from that atmosphere she deliberately made herself "paramountly coolheaded, slow of impulse, and disgustingly practical." But an incident in later life brings out her own thwarted romanticism: she spends an agonized night dreaming of a singer she had almost fallen in love with and realizes that "the dream was no blind chance; it was the expression of something she had kept so close a prisoner that she had never seen it herself; it was the wail from the donjon deeps when the watch slept." She was the daughter of her father after all; but she fights down this revelation of her suppressed self and faces her husband in the morning with her usual imperturbable calm. The story has the air of having been written to demonstrate a thesis, and, though it is organized with skill, it has less life than any of the others in the collection.

"The Marriage of Phaedra," the third of the repudiated stories, is an ambitious tale in Jamesian vein. It tells of an artist's visit to the studio of a fellow artist three years after his death and his discovering there a great, incomplete painting, "The Marriage of Phaedra." The dead artist, Hugh Treffinger, had been an important new influence in art, although since his death his influence had been on the wane and his work misunderstood. The visitor, MacMaster by name, becomes more and more intrigued by Treffinger's work and with the information about Treffinger he is able to get from Treffinger's former "man," James. He decides to write a biography of Treffinger, and this decision brings him into relation with the artist's widow. As the story develops, the truth about Treffinger's relations with his wife gradually emerges, and her misunderstanding of his genius becomes clear. The story ends with the widow's decision to sell "The Marriage of Phaedra" to a dealer in New Zealand and the effect of this decision on MacMaster and James. The situation is full of possibilities, and Miss Cather tries hard to develop them. As usual, the organization is well handled, and the filling in of Treffinger's early history in the middle of the story is done with considerable adroitness. There is a certain self-conscious inflexibility about the story as a whole, however: it has a Jamesian tone without James's suppleness. It never quite reaches out to what it seems to be wanting to say.

The other four stories in *The Troll Garden* were included among the eight stories which made up *Youth and the Bright Medusa,* published in 1920. There were some slight changes, mostly omissions of phrases in order to tighten up a description or the loosening up of a piece of dialogue by substituting a brief, colloquial phrase for a longer and more formal one. On one occasion (in "A Wagner Matinée") a whole paragraph of description is omitted. On another occasion a phrase is

added: this is in "Paul's Case," where in a reference to
Paul's mother Willa Cather has added the significant
phrase "whom Paul could not remember" and thus
provides an important clue to Paul's behavior and character. Though on the whole these changes are quite
minor, it will be fairer to Willa Cather to quote from the
later text of the stories as we discuss them.

The bright Medusa of the title of the 1920 collection
is presumably art itself, with its fascinating and sometimes fatal attraction for youth. The theme that runs
through all these stories is the special status of the artist
in society, the fight of the artist to preserve his integrity
in a world of Philistines, the struggle of sensitivity to
maintain itself in a world of routine and convention.
We have seen this kind of theme handled in *The Song
of the Lark* and *The Professor's House,* and many of
these stories read like sketches for some aspect of one or
the other of these novels or exercises in developing and
presenting this subject.

"Paul's Case," "A Wagner Matinée," "The Sculptor's
Funeral," and "A Death in the Desert" are the stories
reprinted from *The Troll Garden.* Of these "The
Sculptor's Funeral" is the least substantial as a story, but
the most direct expression of a point of view of the
author's. A distinguished modern sculptor, who has
died at the early age of forty, is brought home for burial
to the little Kansas town where he was born and where
his parents still live. His mother is seen to be a hard,
insensitive woman who never understood him or appreciated his gifts. Representatives of the local community
make caustic comments on the dead man's incompetence

in practical matters and gloat over what they consider to be his failure in life. This leads the somewhat bedraggled, drink-worn lawyer, who has understood the dead man and knows what his achievement was and what a triumph it was for the sculptor to have fought free from this atmosphere of petty materialism and squalid censoriousness, to lash out at the citizens in a long harangue which is in fact the central part of the story.

One gets a certain satisfaction in reading this attack on the Philistines; it is effective rhetoric, and the point is well made. But this is Willa Cather proclaiming her faith in art rather than performing as an artist. It is true that many of the incidental touches in this story are admirable—the description of the group waiting at the railroad station, the account of the parlor where the coffin is laid—but the story as a whole is simply an excuse to make a speech; and though it is a good speech it does not in itself make a good story. And the town characters who represent the world of shabby materialism are as conventional caricatures of bourgeois insensitives as ever an art-for-art's-sake writer drew in anti-Philistine wrath.

"Paul's Case" treats of a different aspect of the conflict between sensitivity and drab convention. Paul, a high school student who drives his teachers to distraction by his attitude of almost hysterical contempt, is unable to come to terms with the world of shabby genteel businessmen who set the tone for living in his section of Pittsburgh. A job of ushering at the theatre gives him a glimpse of the plush world of drawing-room drama, and acquaintance with a juvenile actor increases his tendency to live in a theatrical dream world. "Perhaps it was because, in Paul's world, the natural nearly always wore the guise of ugliness, that a certain element of artificiality seemed to him necessary in beauty." He is taken out of school and given a job in a bank, but his drab Pittsburgh life becomes more and more intolerable to him, so that eventually he goes off to New York with a wad of notes and checks stolen from the bank to live a glorious few days at a luxurious hotel. He buys himself expensive clothes, occupies an expensive suite, and fits easily into his new environment. For the first time he loses his nervous, slightly hysterical manner. When he learns from a newspaper that his father has refunded to the bank the amount he had stolen, that the bank has decided not to prosecute "the motherless boy," and that his father is in New York to look for him and bring him back to the intolerable Pittsburgh routine, he commits suicide by throwing himself in front of a train.

"Paul's Case" explores the strange shapes the desire for beauty can take where an atmosphere of genteel ugliness removes all normal opportunities for aesthetic growth and stifles and distorts all natural sensitivities. Again, the point is a conventional one, the attack on the bourgeois world part of a movement which has lost most of its excitement for the modern reader. In these early stories Willa Cather is exploring attitudes and justifying herself as an artist. She displays a fine sense of atmosphere and considerable skill in describing interiors, but these are not yet wholly put at the service of her art. She pounces on situations which symbolize her own need and her own sense of challenging the world, so that sometimes a story turns out a manifesto rather than an effective work of imaginative literature in its own right.

In "A Wagner Matinée" the autobiographical impulse is used more subtly, foreshadowing in some degree the use Miss Cather is to make of it in her midwestern novels. The sense of the remoteness of the Nebraska plains from the urban life of art and sophistication is conveyed in a few deft strokes. The story, told in the first person, is of a visit to the narrator in Boston by his old Aunt Georgiana who had in her youth been a music teacher in the Boston Conservatory but had subsequently eloped with "an idle, shiftless boy of twenty-one," an adventure which led to her "eluding the reproaches of her family and the criticism of her friends by going with him to the Nebraska frontier." They took up a homestead in a remote part of the state and had since lived there in hard-working isolation for thirty years. This is her first return to the East since her elopement.

The narrator is represented as having spent his own childhood with his aunt in Nebraska, and this adds to the sympathetic understanding between writer and subject. He is now taking his aunt to a concert of Wagner music, and the old woman's reaction to this return to a long-lost world of living music is the climax and the main point of the story. Description of the effect of the music on Aunt Georgiana is adroitly woven into the Nebraskan theme, to suggest devices the author was to employ later in *The Song of the Lark:*

Willa Cather

The first number was the *Tannhauser* [*sic*] overture. When the horns drew out the first strain of the Pilgrim's chorus, Aunt Georgiana clutched my coat sleeve. Then it was I first realized that for her this broke a silence of thirty years. With the battle between the two motives, with the frenzy of the Venusberg theme and its ripping of strings, there came to me an overwhelming sense of the waste and wear we are so powerless to combat; and I saw again the tall, naked house on the prairie, black and grim as a wooden fortress; the black pond where I had learned to swim, its margin pitted with sun-dried cattle tracks; the rain gullied clay banks about the naked house, the four dwarf ash seedlings where the dish-cloths were always hung to dry before the kitchen door. The world there was the flat world of the ancients; to the east, a cornfield that stretched to daybreak; to the west, a corral that reached to sunset; between, the conquests of peace, dearer-bought than those of war.

This combination of description and reminiscence is developed through an account of the various items on the program, until Aunt Georgiana is completely over-come and begins to weep quietly. The conclusion brings back Nebraska:

The concert was over; the people filed out of the hall chattering and laughing, glad to relax and find the living level again, but my kinswoman made no effort to rise. The harpist slipped the green felt cover over his instrument; the flute-players shook the water from their mouthpieces; the men of the orchestra went out one by one, leaving the stage to the chairs and music stands, empty as a winter cornfield.

I spoke to my aunt. She burst into tears and sobbed plead-ingly. "I don't want to go, Clark, I don't want to go!"

I understood. For her, just outside the concert hall, lay

the black pond with the cattle-tracked bluffs; the tall, un-painted house, with weather-curled boards, naked as a tower; the crook-backed ash seedlings where the dish-cloths hung to dry; the gaunt, moulting turkeys picking up refuse about the kitchen door.

"A Wagner Matinée" is a slight piece; the structure is simple and the point rather obvious. But it shows Willa Cather developing an original manner, handling a kind of subject she was to make increasingly her own. It has an emotional tone which we find in few of the early stories, a tone which emerges later, triumphantly, in *The Song of the Lark* and *My Ántonia*. The language is handled more plastically than in, say, "The Sculptor's Funeral"; the prose rhythms are subtler and the images more artfully selected and presented. With our knowl-edge of Miss Cather's later work, we can see the sig-nificance of this development in her writing.

"A Death in the Desert" is the most elaborate of the earlier stories in *Youth and the Bright Medusa*. It is the story of a woman singer who, after a brief but trium-phant career, has come home to Cheyenne to die of tuberculosis. Everett Hilgarde, brother of the famous composer Adriance Hilgarde, has also come to Chey-enne, intending to stay very briefly. His remarkable resemblance to his brother has made many people mis-take him for Adriance, as the singer, Katharine Gaylord, does momentarily when she catches a glimpse of him as he alights from the train. Katharine had been in love with Adriance, and they had shared some triumphs to-gether. Now that she is alone and dying, she asks Everett to visit her regularly and talk to her of his brother.

Everett himself had as a young man been in love with Katharine, but shyness and a sense of being unable to reach her glittering world had kept him from making any advances. Now, as he talks with her day after day, she comes gradually to see and admire him for himself, not for his resemblance to his brother, which was the original reason why she asked him to visit her. As they talk, the whole character of Adriance slowly emerges, and the relations between the two men and the singer become clarified. Everett, in spite of important appointments elsewhere, stays with Katharine until her death. As she dies she reverts to her old confusion between Everett and Adriance; looking into Everett's face, she whispers Adriance's name with words of endearment.

This is a more subtly organized story than anything Willa Cather had yet attempted. The theme of the relation between the two brothers—which is a profounder theme in the story than the relation of either of them to Katharine—is developed by oblique strokes very skillfully. The story opens with Everett in the train on the way to Cheyenne: there he is accosted by a passenger who takes him for his brother. This continual confusion between his brother and himself—a purely visual confusion—has a symbolic significance in the story. When Everett and Katharine are talking together he tells more about it:

"I remember, when I was a child I used to be very sensitive about it. I don't think it exactly displeased me, or that I would have had it otherwise, but it seemed like a birthmark, or something not to be lightly spoken of. It came into even my relations with my mother. Ad went abroad to study when he was very young, and mother was all broken up over it. She did her whole duty by each of us, but it was generally understood among us that she'd have made burnt-offerings of us all for him any day. I was a little fellow then, and when she sat alone on the porch on summer evenings, she used sometimes to call me to her and turn my face up in the light that streamed out through the shutters and kiss me, and then I always knew she was thinking of Adriance."

Katharine's sympathy rests on him for a moment before her thoughts move as usual to Adriance. "Poor little chap," she remarks. "How fond people have always been of Adriance! Tell me the latest news of him." As the days go by Everett realizes ever more clearly that

His power to minister to her comfort lay solely in his link with his brother's life. He knew that she sat by him always watching for some trick of gesture, some familiar play of expression, some illusion of light and shadow, in which he should seem wholly Adriance. He knew that she lived upon this, and that in the exhaustion which followed this turmoil of her dying senses, she slept deep and sweet, and dreamed of youth and art and days in a certain old Florentine garden, and not of bitterness and death.

The picture of Adriance that emerges from their conversations and reminiscences is that of a brilliant, restless, charming, selfish creature, who is kind and affectionate and responsive to all handsome women when he is with them but forgets about them when he is away from them. Everett writes to his brother in Europe telling him of Katharine's condition and asking him to write her a letter to cheer her up. Adriance writes the letter. He "always said not only the right thing, but the opportune, graceful, exquisite thing. He caught the lyric essence of the moment, the poetic suggestion of every situation." Miss Cather is wrestling with a theme similar to that handled by Robert Louis Stevenson in *The Master of Ballantrae*—how the enchantingly brilliant character can be of less moral worth than his morally sounder but less fascinating brother. And the theme of the utter—if unconscious—selfishness of the artist as presented, for example, by Bernard Shaw in *The Doctor's Dilemma* is also touched on in this story. Everett, by his generosity and tenderness to the dying Katharine, touches her and wins her warm affection; yet in death she sees him as Adriance.

The story is not perfect, either in structure or texture. But it shows considerable skill in handling a difficult theme, and the manipulation of incident and dialogue shows a finish not previously visible in Willa Cather's work.

The four new stories [1] in *Youth and the Bright Medusa*—"Coming, Aphrodite!" "The Diamond Mine," "A Gold Slipper," and "Scandal"—show no very even progress in technical accomplishment, though they all demonstrate a desire to handle subtler themes than those found in the earliest stories. "A Gold Slipper" is the slenderest of these stories. A businessman is reluctantly dragged by his wife and his wife's friend to a concert given by a distinguished and handsome young woman singer. Circumstances make them traveling companions on the night train to New York immediately

[1] Three of them had appeared in periodicals between 1916 and 1919.

after the concert. In the train she asks him to explain his obvious disapproval of her, and a dialogue ensues in which Philistine and artist confront each other. After their conversation they retire to their respective berths, and in the morning the businessman finds on his berth one of the singer's gold slippers. At first he is annoyed, but on reflection he decides to keep it as a souvenir. The story ends with the businessman, now ill and old, brooding over the tarnished slipper which symbolizes what has forever eluded him—"life and youth." The story is reminiscent of "The Sculptor's Funeral" in that it is contrived to point up the difference between the bourgeois way of life and that of the artist. The singer takes some fine swings at the businessman's attitude and has the last word very effectively. Her point of view is more individual, and her eloquence springs from a more fully realized personality than anything which springs from the wrath of the lawyer in "The Sculptor's Funeral."

"Coming, Aphrodite!" is the story of a painter who lives alone on the top floor of an old house in Washington Square and his relations with an ambitious but callow young woman singer who rents the room next to his. The difference between the painter, who is indifferent to vulgar fame and has consistently avoided stereotyping a style which dealers can recognize and learn to admire, and the singer who is eager for the applause of the world is effectively developed as the progress of their relation is unfolded, yet the story seems rather too loaded with detail to be a thoroughly adequate vehicle for such a theme. Miss Cather becomes interested in the tone and quality of incidental situations and often handles them with skill, but they do not always lead anywhere, or at least they do not always lead to the point where the story seems to be intending to go. The painter and the budding singer have a love affair, which comes abruptly to an end when the painter realizes that the singer is trying to help him by securing for him the patronage of a successful "popular" artist whom he despises. The story ends (like so many of Willa Cather's) with the return of the singer to New York many years later, after she has achieved fame in Europe and America. There she inquires of a picture dealer whether the painter has achieved any reputation, and he replies: "He is a great name with all the young men, and he is decidedly an influence in art. But one can't definitely place a man who is original, erratic, and who is changing all the time." Satisfied that her former lover has achieved a real reputation in his way, she remarks that "one doesn't like to have been an utter fool, even at twenty" and retires to her car where her face resumes its "hard and settled" look. "Tomorrow night . . . this mask would be the golden face of Aphrodite. But a 'big' career takes its toll, even with the best of luck." So the story concludes, as though its theme were the toll that art takes of its practitioners, whereas in fact its theme is much broader than that, involving the difference between two kinds of character and two kinds of artists and the relation of each to society.

"The Diamond Mine" is also the story of a singer— a successful singer who is resented and exploited by her family. This is one of the most interesting stories in the collection: the theme is more original, and the structure is more complex than they are in any of the other stories in this volume. Miss Cather employs her favorite device of the flash back with considerable skill, maneuvering the story around the heroine's relationship with her third husband, the Bohemian violinist and composer Blasius Bouchalka. The story, told in the first person by a friend of the heroine, opens on board ship, with Cressida Garnet, the singer, on her way to Europe. Conversations between Cressida and the narrator, between the narrator and Cressida's accompanist, Miletus Poppas, between Cressida and her son Horace, interspersed with explanatory recollections by the narrator, gradually build up a picture of Cressida's career and of her relations with her jealous, sponging family, for whom, as for so many others, she is merely "the diamond mine." The skill with which comment and dialogue are alternated shows a maturing technique.

The second part of the story gives the narrator's recollections of Cressida's early life, and this works up inevitably to her marriage with Bouchalka, the story of which occupies the third section. Bouchalka had been a gifted but impoverished musician whom Cressida discovered lost in New York, helped, and then married. After some years of happy marriage she returned home once unexpectedly to find him in bed with the Bohemian cook, and Cressida, who "knew herself too well to attempt a readjustment," divorced him forthwith, leaving him bewildered by her attitude but unreproachful.

It is a sadly ironical little episode. Bouchalka was in many ways an excellent husband for Cressida, and he continued to adore her; a difference in moral temperament forced them apart. Cressida's fourth and last husband was the least successful of all; he was rapacious, and lost her money in ambitious but unsuccessful investments. The final section of the story briefly tells of her last marriage and brings the narrative forward to Cressida's death, setting her whole life now back in the past. Her relatives, outraged that she left so little, nevertheless squabbled over her will, and, contesting her bequest of fifty thousand dollars to the faithful Poppas, had her old letters read in court in an attempt to prove that Cressida had always intended to leave them her money:

Such letters they were! The writing of a tired, overdriven woman; promising money, sending money herewith, asking for an acknowledgment of the draft sent last month, etc. In the letters to Jerome Brown she begged for information about his affairs and entreated him to go with her to some foreign city where they could live quietly and where she could rest; if they were careful, there would "be enough for all." Neither Brown nor her brothers and sisters had any sense of shame about these letters. It seemed never to occur to them that this golden stream, whether it rushed or whether it trickled, came out of the industry, out of the mortal body of a woman. They regarded her as a natural source of wealth; a copper vein, a diamond mine.

The story ends with a glimpse of Poppas, in retirement in "the middle of Asia."

This is a well-manipulated narrative, with an unconventional handling of chronology subordinated at all points to the needs of the main theme and to the establishment of the appropriate tone. The tone is ironical and melancholy, but not in the least cynical. Willa

Cather had attempted this tone before (it is a difficult tone to achieve with any success) but here for the first time in a story about the life of art she goes beyond making a point about the relation of the artist's way to other ways of life to project with considerable richness of texture a pattern of attitudes, hopes, achievements, and frustrations.

Willa Cather's next collection of short stories was published in 1932 under the title *Obscure Destinies*. This contained three stories: "Neighbour [2] Rosicky" (written in 1928 and first published, like so many of her stories, in a magazine), "Old Mrs. Harris," and "Two Friends," both written in 1931. In these stories she is handling themes which for the most part she had already left behind in her novels. She is drawing on her Nebraska memories and other recollections of her childhood, and the richness of texture and clear emotional pattern which the autobiographical impulse gave to *O Pioneers!* and *My Antonia* are to be found here also. She is no longer writing about artists: there is something inbred about writers choosing fellow artists as themes, and Willa Cather seems eventually to have realized this. Nor do we find here the note of self-conscious belligerence about the status of the artist that dominates her early work. These stories are essentially studies in the quality of country living in the American Midwest and West, done with an affectionate interest in the human characters involved and a lyrical sense of the natural background.

"Neighbour Rosicky" is a character sketch projected

[2] Miss Cather seems always to have used the British "—our" spelling in this and similar words.

through the arrangement of symbolic incidents. The last years of this wise and kindly old Czech farmer in Nebraska are described so as to develop a sense of what such a life stood for in terms of a satisfactory adjustment to the demands both of nature and of one's fellow men. Its earthiness almost neutralizes the incipient sentimentality, and the relation of the action to its context in agricultural life gives the story an elemental quality that is lacking in the thinner accounts of the artist's life that we find in *Youth and the Bright Medusa*. The story opens with Rosicky in the doctor's office, being told to take things easy because he has a weak heart, and it ends with his death after he has ignored the doctor's advice by raking thistles out of an alfalfa field. Between these limits Miss Cather manages to present all that was significant in the man's whole life and, in addition, to handle a specific theme—the old man's relation to his city-bred daughter-in-law—so as to focus the larger meanings. One of the most obvious pieces of "Americana" among Miss Cather's stories, "Neighbour Rosicky" has appealed to conventional taste in a way that her more original work has sometimes failed to do.

The second story, "Old Mrs. Harris," is the longest and most substantial in the book. It is the study of a southern family who have moved to a small town in the West and find that the pattern of family living they bring with them is misunderstood and resented by their new neighbors. Old Mrs. Harris has left her comfortable southern home to follow the fortunes of her married daughter: she regards it her duty, as an old woman, to do all she can to enable the younger generation to live in as carefree a manner as possible, and that point of view is accepted as a complete matter of course by her daughter Victoria, who allows her mother to act the part of family drudge (as it seems to the neighbors) without any awareness of doing wrong. The nature and results of this situation are explored in the story with considerable cunning and with most effective deployment of incident.

We first see Mrs. Harris through the eyes of Mrs. David Rosen, an intelligent and well-educated Jewish woman whose husband "didn't mind keeping a clothing-store in a little Western town, so long as he had a great deal of time to read philosophy." The Rosens represent a standard of culture and of cultured living unique in the little town of Skyline, though we are not told this about them until later on in the story. Mrs. Rosen has long planned to call on Mrs. Harris some time when she can find her alone, but has hitherto been prevented by Victoria's arrangements. This time she sees Victoria leave, then runs over with a pot of coffee and some coffee cake to ask Mrs. Harris to join her in her afternoon coffee. The result disconcerts her: Grandma Harris does not respond. "Receiving a visitor alone, unsupervised by her daughter, having cake and coffee that should properly be saved for Victoria, was all so irregular that Mrs. Harris could not enjoy it. Mrs. Rosen doubted if she tasted the cake as she swallowed it,—certainly she ate it without relish, as a hollow form." Willa Cather pauses at this point to describe the "hideous, cluttered room" in which they were sitting—

a room which particularly offended Mrs. Rosen, who "liked order and comeliness so much":

> A walnut table stood against a blind window, piled high with old magazines and tattered books, and children's caps and coats. There was a wash-stand (two wash-stands, if you counted the oilcloth-covered box as one). A corner of the room was curtained off with some black-and-red-striped cotton goods, for a clothes closet. In another corner was the wooden lounge with a thin mattress and a red calico spread which was Grandma's bed. Beside it was her wooden rocking-chair, and the little splint-bottom chair with the legs sawed short on which her darning-basket usually stood, but which Mrs. Rosen was now using for a tea-table.

The picking out of these details at this point in the story shows that awareness of the need to build up the emotional tone of a narrative by the proper distribution of symbolic objects—an awareness which Willa Cather displays so effectively in her mature work.

As the two ladies talk, the cat comes in, and Mrs. Rosen notices how affectionately Mrs. Harris handles it; then the grandchildren come home from school, and an atmosphere of cheerful affection breaks in, quite different from anything that Mrs. Rosen's preconceptions about Mrs. Harris' function in the family might have led her to expect. Just after Mrs. Rosen leaves, Victoria (Mrs. Templeton) comes home, and what follows is equally illuminating:

> Mrs. Templeton stopped by the picket fence to smile at the children playing in the back yard,—and it was a real smile, she was glad to see them. She called Ronald over to the fence to give him a kiss. He was hot and sticky.

"Was your teacher nice today? Now run in and ask Grandma to wash your face and put a clean waist on you."

Grandma does all the dirty work; yet Victoria is not the spoilt and selfish woman one might suppose, Grandma does not in the least regard herself as ill-used, and everybody in the family is courteous and well-behaved. Having so far seen the Harris family only through Mrs. Rosen's eyes, we are still puzzled by the seeming contradictions in this state of affairs. In the second section of the story, which now begins, Miss Cather adroitly shifts the point of view and gives us a direct description of the Harrises at home.

This second section concentrates on Mrs. Harris, and while it emphasizes her weariness and scant physical comforts, it also shows the other side:

She did not regret her decision; indeed, there had been no decision. Victoria had never once thought it possible that Ma should not go wherever she and the children went, and Mrs. Harris had never thought it possible. Of course she regretted Tennessee, though she would never admit it to Mrs. Rosen:—the old neighbours, the yard and garden she had worked in all her life, the apple trees she had planted, the lilac arbour, tall enough to walk in, which she had clipped and shaped so many years.

Old women, Mrs. Harris believed, "were tied to the chariot of young life, and had to go where it went, because they were needed." She did not regard her lot as requiring pity. And as for Victoria—"if Victoria once suspected Mrs. Rosen's indignation, it would be all over. She would freeze her neighbour out, and that friendly voice, that quick pleasant chatter with the little foreign twist, would thenceforth be heard only at a distance, in the alley-way or across the fence. Victoria had a good heart, but she was terribly proud and could not bear the least criticism."

The third section introduces Vickie, Mrs. Harris' eldest grandchild, Victoria's daughter. She is working for a scholarship and comes into the Rosens' house to read and to receive encouragement in her educational ambitions. This gives a new turn to the story, providing an element of plot (hitherto we have had mostly the static situation and the character sketch) which is to be used to throw new light on the situation already presented and to project the story structurally to a satisfactory conclusion. We leave Vickie reading in the parlor while Miss Cather focuses on Mrs. Rosen and tells in retrospect the story of her relations with Victoria Templeton. This kind of handling of chronology—describing the present situation, then back to the past to show in some degree how it developed, then to the present again to show something new, then some more illumination from the past—can be irritating and confusing in inexpert hands; but Willa Cather knows what she is doing. It is a kind of mystery story, the mystery to be solved being the true character of Grandma Harris and her relation to her family. Mrs. Rosen tries to play the detective, but, as in all good mystery stories, it is not the official detective who solves the mystery. No individual, in fact, solves it, unless it be the reader, who, presented with the growing complexity of the situation, eventually sees a pattern rich enough to contain all the disparate elements. The movement back and forth in time helps to enrich the pattern until we can see in it all that we need to see.

The fourth section of the story brings Victoria into a social context in order to exhibit the other side of her nature (nurtured for society, she is seen at her best in relation to people outside her own family) and to show some of her fellow townspeople, resenting this fact in her upbringing and her behavior, exhibiting their malice. There is a conflict between the mores bred by southern standards of gentility and the rough democracy of a bustling little western town. Miss Cather takes no sides; she deploys her material cunningly, and lets the situation explain itself.

In the fifth section we are back with Mrs. Harris, exploring her background and the circumstances of her earlier life. The previous history of the Templetons is then fully related; it is shown how unsuccessful projects of Mr. Templeton's had finally landed them in this little western town, what a blind alley such a situation was for them, and how they strove to keep up the old life in increasingly discouraging circumstances. The brightest part of the picture is Mrs. Harris' relations with her grandchildren; here something of the old southern clan sense, the sense of the organic unity of the family, is preserved:

Sometimes, in the morning, if her feet ached more than usual, Mrs. Harris felt a little low. . . . She would hang up her towel with a sigh and go into the kitchen, feeling that it was hard to make a start. But the moment she heard the children running down the uncarpeted back stairs, she forgot to be low. Indeed, she ceased to be an individual, an old woman with aching feet; she became part of a group, became a relationship. She was drunk up into their freshness when they burst in upon her, telling her about their dreams, explaining their troubles with buttons and shoe-laces and underwear shrunk too small. The tired, solitary old woman Grandmother had been at daybreak vanished; suddenly the morning seemed as important to her as it did to the children, and the mornings ahead stretched out sunshiny, important.

The death of the cat and the reactions to this event of the various members of the Templeton family throw new light both on Mrs. Harris and her daughter. We have been prepared for the symbolic use of the cat by the first section, when the animal's appearance brought out more warmth from Mrs. Harris than any other single incident. Mrs. Harris' fierce resentment of her daughter's suggestion that the dead cat be thrown out on the trash pile and her conspiracy with her grand-children to give it decent burial reveal that after all there were some basic differences between mother and daughter; yet Victoria's surprising gentleness with the children when she learns that they have deceived her at once prevents us from making too facile an interpretation of this difference. The clues to the solution of the mystery are strewn ever more thickly, but by this time it is ceasing to be a special mystery on its own and is becoming recognizable as part of the larger mystery of personality, of human nature, of life itself.

The concluding sections of the story are taken up with Vickie's attempt to win a competitive scholarship

to the University of Michigan. She is successful but
learns soon after that the scholarship would only pay
part of her expenses; she would have to provide three
hundred dollars more herself. This Mr. Templeton
professes himself unable to do: he tells Vickie kindly
but firmly that he just has not got the money. A crisis
ensues. The problem is solved privately by Mrs. Harris,
who, emerging for the first time as an independent individual, arranges with the Rosens for a loan to Vickie of
the necessary money. In that final interview between
Mrs. Harris and Mrs. Rosen (deliberately and instruc-
tively contrasted with that first interview with which
the story opens), each sees and appreciates the other
more clearly, and Mrs. Harris, now that she is acting as
an individual and determining her own relation to her
granddaughter, can at last understand and respond to
Mrs. Rosen's affection.

Meanwhile confusion is reigning in the Templeton
household. Victoria discovers that she is pregnant
again and is depressed and hopeless. Mr. Templeton
goes off on a business trip. Mrs. Harris, having risen to
her great moment, takes to her bed in what she knows
is her last illness. Vickie learns the good news, unaware
whom she has to thank for it. Grandma is left alone with
the younger grandchildren, the two twins, with whom
she has achieved a perfect relationship. That night she
loses consciousness and never regains it.

The pattern is not complete yet; Victoria and Vickie
are left *in medias res*. But patterns which involve different generations are never complete; all the author has
to do is to show them as sufficiently rich to illustrate the

continuity of the design and the relevance of what at first appear to be isolated elements. "Old Mrs. Harris," the longest and most originally constructed of Willa Cather's short stories, is her most successful attempt to achieve this kind of pattern on this scale.

"Two Friends," the final story in *Obscure Destinies,* is a much slighter affair. It is cast in the form of a reminiscence and tells the story of two friends who lived "in a little wooden town in a shallow Kansas river valley." One was a banker and one was a big cattleman, and in spite of differences in background and temperament there was a deep affection between them. They spent every summer evening sitting side by side on two armchairs on the wooden sidewalk outside the banker's store and talked together. The flavor and quality of their talk and of their personalities are presented through anecdotal retrospect, and a tone of easy informality pervades the narrative. As usual, Miss Cather picks out the significant detail in describing the background, building up the atmosphere through the proper use of symbolic properties.

The narrator (a youngster at the time of these events) reveals himself only occasionally and in such a way as to provide a nostalgic tone to the reminiscence. "I liked to listen to those two because theirs was the only 'conversation' one could hear about the streets." "I suppose there were moonless nights, and dark ones with but a silver shaving and pale stars in the sky, just as in the spring. But I remember them all as flooded by the rich indolence of a full moon, or a half-moon set in uncertain blue."

The sketch ends with an account of how the two friends moved apart. Dillon was in Chicago at the time when the Democratic convention first nominated William Jennings Bryan, and he came back full of enthusiasm for the great orator. Trueman, who regarded Bryan as a "great windbag," could not conceal his contempt, and thus Bryan drove the two friends apart. When Trueman, believing that Dillon's enthusiastic harangues in support of Bryan were "no way for a banker to talk," at last withdrew his account from Dillon's bank, the rift was complete. For the narrator, nothing was the same in that small Kansas town again.

Dillon died suddenly soon afterwards, and Trueman departed for San Francisco. The personal note is sounded most strongly in the conclusion:

The breaking-up of that friendship between two men who scarcely noticed my existence was a real loss to me, and has ever since been a regret. More than once, in Southern countries where there is a smell of dust and dryness in the air and the nights are intense, I have come upon a stretch of dusty white road drinking up the moonlight beside a blind wall, and have felt a sudden sadness. Perhaps it was not until the next morning that I knew why,—and then only because I had dreamed of Mr. Dillon or Mr. Trueman in my sleep. When that old scar is occasionally touched by chance, it rouses the old uneasiness; the feeling of something broken that could so easily have been mended; of something delightful that was senselessly wasted, of a truth that was accidentally distorted—one of the truths we want to keep.

Willa Cather

The story is slight enough, but it has tone and atmosphere, both achieved in a manner characteristic of Willa Cather.

Willa Cather's last book of short stories, *The Old Beauty and Others*, published posthumously in 1948, contains three pieces, none of them representing her best work. The title story tells of an old woman who had once been a famous beauty and the friend of great men but who is now in retirement at Aix-les-Bains. The story of her life is told in some ingenious flash backs, and we learn how her husband had discovered her in Martinique and brought her home to London, where her popularity had aroused his jealousy to the point where he eventually arranged a divorce. Her later successes, under the patronage of "a succession of Great Protectors," are briefly indicated, and we return to the present, to 1922 in Aix-les-Bains, where, old and no longer beautiful, she is living with a companion in a hotel, trying in vain to recapture something of the flavor of prewar European civilization, especially of the spacious days of Queen Victoria's later years. Occupying an important place in the story as observer and fellow *laudator temporis acti* is Henry Seabury, fifty-five years old, "American-born, educated in England." He had known Lady Longstreet in her heyday and had, in fact, on one critical occasion in New York (duly recorded in a flash back), saved her from rape by a *nouveau riche* immigrant with a foreign accent; he has returned from many years in China to find the old Europe gone, surviving only (in some degree) in Aix-les-Bains, where he accordingly decides to stay. He and Lady Longstreet talk of the past together, until her sudden death after a motor ride in which they almost collided with two very vulgar American tourists "clad in dirty white knickers and sweaters." The shock of this violent confrontation with the postwar generation was too much for the old beauty, who passed away in her sleep that night.

Any brief summary of the story is bound to sound silly but only a little sillier than the story itself. It is, in fact, a preposterous tale, full of the most violent clichés and the most stagy situations. It is difficult to believe that Willa Cather meant it seriously: it reads like a parody.

A great deal can be done, of course, with the nostalgia of people who have outlived the world to which they belong. It is a potentially tragic, or at least an elegiac, theme, and if handled by an author who is in sympathy with the lost civilization sought for in vain by the hero or heroine, can achieve a richly plangent quality. One does not object to "The Old Beauty" because its principal characters idealize a past age, or for its satire of European and American manners after the first World War, but for the complete lack of conviction in both characters and situations, the empty theatricality of the dialogue, the peevish pathos of the tone. There are some effective touches, a brief description here, a perceptive remark there, but on the whole there is little to suggest that here is a master at work. Willa Cather's disillusion with the world around her and with all the literary and political movements which had grown up in her own adult life seems to have finally led her to a state of tawdry nostalgia which corrupted her art.

On her native heath she did better. "The Best Years," the second story in this collection and the last story she wrote, is set in the Nebraska farm country of her early books. It is a slight enough piece, but it has a mournful charm that is not to be found in anything else she had written. It begins in 1899, with Miss Evangeline Knightly, County Superintendent of Public Instruction, "driving through the beautiful Nebraska land which lies between the Platte River and the Kansas line." Miss Knightly takes us to Lesley Ferguesson, the charming young schoolteacher in the little one-story school house at Wild Rose. The account of Lesley and of her relations with the sympathetic and attractive Miss Knightly has a fine pastoral freshness. Nostalgia has here added charm and innocence rather than faded splendor to an ideally remembered situation. From the schoolhouse the story takes us to Lesley with her parents and brothers at home, and here there is a frankly sentimental, yet withal a fascinatingly persuasive, picture of an ideal farmer's family basking in domestic affections. This is in the purest pastoral tradition, and as pastoral it is successful. The middle section of the story tells us of young Lesley's sudden death from pneumonia contracted during the great blizzard; and the final section takes us twenty years forward, with Miss Knightly (now Mrs. Thorndike) revisiting her native haunts and meeting Mrs. Ferguesson for the first time since her daughter's death. The Ferguessons are well off now and inhabit a fine new house, but Mrs. Ferguesson is nostalgic for "the old house down by the depot" and the warm family life they had led there when the children were young. On that note of pastoral elegy the story ends.

The whole force of the story depends on the early picture of Lesley and of the central place she took in the family. The fourteen-year-old schoolteacher, idolized by her younger brothers and adored by the older brother Hector, admired and depended on by her parents, is described with a passionate tenderness far different from the more objective understanding with which Alexandra Bergson or Ántonia were presented. Like Ántonia she is a rustic goddess, but not an Earth Mother, not Ceres but rather Proserpine, who, like the original Proserpine

<blockquote>
gathering flowers
Herself a fairer flower by gloomy Dis
Was gathered.
</blockquote>

She is the symbol of all the lost innocence that to Willa Cather in her last years seemed to have vanished from the earth, and the perfect affection which united the family gathered around her was similarly bathed in the glory of a lost world. The family twenty years later, rich, conventional, and uncomfortable, represents, one might almost say, man after the Fall: the earlier scenes had a prelapsarian quality about them.

"Before Breakfast," the concluding story in this volume, is the slightest of the three. It is the story of a self-educated businessman on holiday in his favorite little Canadian island, where he goes to be away from his

superior wife and grown-up sons. He is a rather improbable character, who reads Scott, Dickens, Fielding,
and Shakespeare for pleasure, to the cold astonishment
of his professor son, yet belligerently announces that he
is going to hear John McCormack sing "Kathleen
Mavourneen" when his wife and son start discussing
Koussevitzky's handling of Brahms' *Second Symphony.*
We see him meditating these things alone on his island,
having been somewhat shaken by his encounter with a
geologist and his attractive daughter on his way to the
island. An early morning walk and a glimpse of the
geologist's daughter out for a swim restore his assurance,
shattered earlier by the geologist's revelation of the vast
age of the island. But now he is no longer troubled by
such cosmic imaginings. "He was walking fast down the
winding trails. Everything since he left the cabin had
been reassuring, delightful—everything was the same,
and so was he!" He comes into the cabin for breakfast,
chuckling to himself: "Anyhow, when that first am-
phibious frog-toad found his water-hole dried up behind him, and jumped out to hop along till he could
find another—well, he started on a long hop." This is
in the category of what *The New Yorker* would call
"chuckles we doubt ever got chuckled."

The interest of the story—which is really a sketch
for a story rather than a completed work—lies in its
reversal of the roles of the businessman and the professor. This time it is the businessman who reads Scott
and Shakespeare and is disturbed by the cold brilliance
of his academic son as well as by his socially superior
wife. It is almost *The Professor's House* turned upside

down. What led Miss Cather to reverse one of her favorite symbols in this late story is impossible to tell; but it is worth noting that in the midst of all her disillusion with modern life and nostalgia for the past she found time to create, late in her career, one wholly sympathetic American businessman.

The Old Beauty and Others is thick with nostalgia. Everybody in the stories who is worth anything escapes or tries to escape from the modern world. Miss Cather had moved steadily away from contemporary life as her work progressed, and in her last work she reached the point at which this movement injured her art. This is not to say that an artist must stick to the contemporary world to be effective, but only that not all forms of escape from it are artistically profitable. Walter Scott, who in his best novels explored the mutations of the heroic ideal as it survived into a commercial age, was motivated by an attitude not dissimilar to Willa Cather's, but he used his nostalgia to develop a creative tension between the ideal and the possible. Miss Cather, who in her essay "Escapism" in 1936 fiercely maintained that all art is escape, must have been aware in some degree of what she was doing, yet she cannot have altogether realized what this harping on the escapist theme was doing to her art. In collecting a group of essays under the title *Not under Forty* in 1936, she explained that she meant that "the book will have little interest for people under forty years of age. The world broke in two in 1922 or thereabouts, and the persons and prejudices recalled in these sketches slid back into yesterday's seven thousand years." This belligerent insistence that she had nothing to say to the younger generation reflects an odd state of mind and one which is not healthy in a novelist. Perhaps the faults of her last stories derive from the fact that she became too self-consciously old-fashioned, an attitude which may sometimes be as harmful as that of the too self-conscious *avant garde*.

CHAPTER 7

Final Estimate

BEFORE we attempt to sum up Willa Cather's achievement as a novelist, some reference should be made to her poetry and miscellaneous writings, which, if they did not conspicuously add to her reputation, are nevertheless of interest to students of her mind and art.

Willa Cather's first published book was a "slim volume" of verse, and throughout her life she continued sporadically to write poetry. *April Twilights*, first published in 1903, was reissued in 1923 together with thirteen later poems which had meanwhile appeared in magazines. Her total poetic output, however, remained small, and her work in this medium never achieved the distinction of her prose fiction. She displayed, even in her undergraduate contributions to the *Hesperian*, an ability to handle competently traditional metrical forms and some real skill with the elegiac cadence. Some of the poems of the 1903 volume are occasionally reminiscent of the controlled plangency of Emily Brontë's poetry, but they have not Emily Brontë's strange intensity. Such a poem as "In Media Vita" is not unskillful, in spite of its romantic slackness, but it lacks what Hop-

kins called "inscape," that passionate individuality that
gives a poem its own unique life:

> Streams of the spring a-singing,
>   Winds of the May that blow,
> Birds from the Southland winging,
>   Buds in the grasses below.
> Clouds that speed hurrying over,
>   And the climbing rose by the wall,
> Singing of bees in the clover,
>   And the dead, under all!

This was a favorite meter of Miss Cather's, and a favorite mood. We see it again in "Winter at Delphi":

> Cold are the stars of the night,
>   Wild is the tempest crying,
> Fast through the velvet dark
>   Little white flakes are flying.
> Still is the House of Song.
>   But the fire on the hearth is burning;
> And the lamps are trimmed, and the cup
>   Is full for his day of returning.
> His watchers are fallen asleep,
>   They wait but his call to follow,
> Ay, to the ends of the earth—
>   But Apollo, the god, Apollo?

Some of the poems ("Poppies on Ludlow Castle," for
example) suggest A. E. Housman in subject, mood, and
rhythms: the almost melodramatic sense of pity that we
find in Housman was an indulgence Miss Cather al-

lowed herself in her verse only—there is no trace of it in the novels. Closer to the novels in tone and feeling are the purely descriptive poems, of which the brief "Prairie Dawn" is perhaps the best:

> A crimson fire that vanquishes the stars;
> A pungent odor from the dusty sage;
> A sudden stirring of the huddle herds;
> A breaking of the distant table-lands
> Through purple mists ascending, and the flare
> Of water-ditches silver in the light;
> A swift, bright lance hurled low across the world;
> A sudden sickness for the hills of home.

The later poems sometimes show greater metrical flexibility and fewer of the conventional romantic properties, yet give no indication that their author was aware of any of the new movements that were afoot in both American and English poetry. "The Palatine" has echoes of Rossetti, and reads as though it were written about 1870:

> "Have you been with the King to Rome,
>   Brother, big brother?"
> "I've been there and I've come home.
>   Back to your play, little brother."

> "Oh, how high is Caesar's house,
>   Brother, big brother?"
> "Goats about the doorways browse:
> Night hawks nest in the burnt roof-tree,
> Home of the wild bird and home of the bee."

Willa Cather

"The Swedish Mother," however, is more original
and more clearly related to the themes of the novels.
Miss Cather is attempting a realistic narrative verse:

> *On the kitchen doorstep low*
> *Sat a Swedish mother;*
> *In her arms one baby slept,*
> *By her sat another.*

> "All time, 'way back in old countree,
> Your grandpa, he been good to me.
> Your grandpa, he been young man, too,
> And I been yust li'l' girl, like you.
> All time in spring, when evening come,
> We go bring sheep an' li'l' lambs home.
> We go big field, 'way up on hill,
> Ten times high like our windmill.
> One time your grandpa leave me wait
> While he call sheep down. By de gate
> I sit still till night come dark. . . ."

The use of Swedish dialect in a narrative verse of
octosyllabic couplets has a curiously stilted effect, and
the experiment, while interesting, can hardly be called
successful. The conclusion restores the lyrical note, and
tries to put the story in its proper emotional context:

> *Every night the red-haired child*
> *Begs to hear the story,*
> *When the pasture ridges burn*
> *With the sunset glory.*

> *She can never understand,*
> *Since the tale ends gladly,*

Final Estimate

Why her mother, telling it,
Always smiles so sadly.

Wonderingly she looks away
Where her mother's gazing;
Only sees the drifting herd,
In the sunset grazing.

This is the kind of thing she did better in her short stories.

Spanish Johnny, who figures in *The Song of the Lark,* appears in an autobiographical poem:

> The old West, the old time,
>   The old wind singing through
> The red, red grass a thousand miles,
>   And, Spanish Johnny, you!
> He'd sit beside the water-ditch
>   When all his herd was in,
> And never mind a child, but sing
>   To his mandolin.

There is a faded conventionality about this and similar poems which we never find in her prose. Occasionally Miss Cather breaks away from regular metrical forms into a freer idiom to produce a kind of prose poetry which seems to be struggling for the freedom and flexibility of real prose:

> Evening and the flat land,
> Rich and somber and always silent;
> The miles of fresh-plowed soil,
> Heavy and black, full of strength and harshness;

Willa Cather

The growing wheat, the growing weeds,
The toiling horses, the tired men . . .

"Macon Prairie" and "A Silver Cup" are narrative poems told in a monotonous blank verse with consistently "feminine" endings. More interesting is "Poor Marty," described as "a lament for Martha, the old kitchenmaid, by her fellow servant, the stableman." This has a lilt to it and a suggestion of a folk quality, and in its simple way it is not unsuccessful:

Who will scour the pots and pans,
Now Marty's gone away?
Who will scald the milking cans
And put the cream away?
Who will wash the goblets tall,
And chiney plates along the wall,
Platters big and platters small,
Never let one crack or fall,
Now Marty's gone away?
Ding-dong-dell, ding-dong-dell, poor Marty's gone away.

The poems of a distinguished novelist are always interesting as revealing the author's moods and attitudes more directly than is generally done in prose fiction, whatever their intrinsic merit as poems. Miss Cather's verses possess this interest, and some of them are in addition agreeable and competent exercises in a medium which was not really hers. She was essentially a prose writer: even her least satisfactory novels and stories show her handling prose with a control and an assurance, a firm clarity of style and a craftsmanlike directness which she never displays in verse in anything like the same degree.

Some of her best prose is in "occasional" pieces—sketches, reminiscences, criticism—which she wrote for various periodicals. Her appreciation of Sarah Orne Jewett, her reminiscences of Mrs. James Fields and her house in Charles Street, her account of her meeting with Flaubert's niece in Aix-les-Bains have a happy luminosity of style which combines an almost matter-of-fact precision with the ability to set going carefully modulated overtones. This is journalism, perhaps, but journalism raised to the level of art:

When the door at 148 Charles Street was opened we waited a few moments in a small reception-room just off the hall, then went up a steep, thickly carpeted stairway and entered the "long drawing room," where Mrs. Fields and Miss Jewett sat at tea. That room ran the depth of the house, its front windows, heavily curtained, on Charles Street, its back windows looking down on a deep garden. Directly above the garden wall lay the Charles River and, beyond, the Cambridge shore. At five o'clock in the afternoon the river was silvery from a half-hidden sun; over the great open space of water the western sky was dove-coloured with little ripples of rose. The air was full of soft moisture and the hint of approaching spring. Against this screen of pale winter light were the two ladies: Mrs. Fields reclining on a green sofa, directly under the youthful portrait of Charles Dickens (now in the Boston Art Museum), Miss Jewett seated, the low tea-table between them.

Or consider this, from her account of her meeting with Flaubert's niece:

The next morning I told Madame Grout that, because of the illness of a friend, I must start at once for Paris.

And when, she asked, could I return and go south to Antibes and the Villa Tanit, to see her Flaubert collection, and the interior of his study, which she had brought down there thirty-five years ago?

I told her I was afraid that visit must be put off until next summer.

She gave a very charming laugh. "At my age, of course, the future is somewhat uncertain!" Then she asked whether, on her return to Antibes, she could send me some souvenir of our meeting; would I like to have something that had belonged to her uncle, or some letter written by him?

I told her that I was not a collector; that manuscripts and autographed letters meant very little to me. The things of her uncle that were valuable to me I already had, and had had for years. It rather hurt me that she should think I wanted any material reminder of her or of Flaubert. It was the Flaubert in her mind and heart that was to give me a beautiful memory.

On the following day, at *déjeuner,* I said good-bye to Madame Grout; I was leaving on the two o'clock train. It was a hurried and mournful parting, but there was real feeling on both sides. She had counted upon my staying longer, she said. But she did not for a moment take on a slightly aggrieved tone, as many privileged old ladies would have done. There was nothing "wayward" or self-indulgent about Madame Grout; the whole discipline of her life had been to the contrary. One had one's objective, and one went toward it; one had one's duty, and one did it as best one could.

The last glimpse I had of her was as she stood in the

dining-room, the powder on her face quite destroyed by tears, her features agitated, but her head erect and her eyes flashing. And the last words I heard from her expressed a hope that I would always remember the pleasure we had had together in talking unreservedly about *les œuvres de mon oncle.* Standing there, she seemed holding to that name as to a staff. A great memory and a great devotion were the things she lived upon, certainly; they were her armour against a world concerned with insignificant matters.

The concluding generalization here (to pick out only one point) is handled with a fine deftness. Consider the placing of that "certainly" in the last sentence, and the effectiveness of the French phrase "les œuvres de mon oncle" in the sentence preceding it. This last paragraph is made up of longer sentences than the other, for the incident is rising toward its conclusion, and the emotion is expanding. Yet when Miss Cather reaches the culminating simile, it stands starkly in the one short sentence in the paragraph—"Standing there, she seemed holding to that name as to a staff"—for any swelling of rhythms at this point would soften the effect, would make the sentence obviously emotional, and so spoil the perfect discipline with which the prose is handled. If this short sentence were allowed to end the paragraph, the conclusion would come with too great a snap; so the ending comes with a longer, carefully balanced sentence, drawing the incident gently to a close.

Her critical essays often illuminate her own view of the artist's function and procedures. Here, for example, is a remark on this general subject from her essay on Miss Jewett:

The artist spends a lifetime in pursuing the things that haunt him, in having his mind "teased" by them, in trying to get these conceptions down on paper exactly as they are to him and not in conventional poses supposed to reveal their character; trying this method and that, as a painter tries different lightings and different attitudes with his subject to catch the one that presents it more suggestively than any other. And at the end of a lifetime he emerges with much that is more or less happy experimenting, and comparatively little that is the very flower of himself and his genius.

Throughout her career as a novelist Miss Cather pursued the subjects that "teased" her mind. We have seen how this led her from novels set in Nebraska in which she recaptures impressions acquired in her childhood through studies of the impact of a commercial civilization on a sensitive personality to a discovery of those picturesque areas of history where sensitivity and heroism could exist together. It led her, too, more and more away from her generation and away from the new and lively influences that were coming into literature after the first World War. She wrote appreciatively of Katharine Mansfield, but what impressed her most about Miss Mansfield's work was her desire to recapture in her stories the quality of her childhood life in New Zealand. Her one critical remark about D. H. Lawrence is contemptuous. She defends her praise of Thomas Mann's Joseph series by insisting that, while the contemporary critics were "concerned only with his for-wardness," Mann "also goes back a long way, and his backwardness is more gratifying to the backward"—and among the backward she includes herself.

It is odd that her early Populist sympathies, which led her to be ever more suspicious of modern industrial America, should have ended by making her a nostalgic idealizer of the past. Writing in 1936 of Mrs. Fields and Sarah Orne Jewett, she bewails the change that had come over the literary scene since the days when 148 Charles Street echoed to the conversation of the Victorian giants. "The English classes, we are told, can be 'interested' only in contemporary writers, the newer the better." She asks herself how this lamentable change can be explained:

Just how did this change come about, one wonders. When and where were the Arnolds overthrown and the Brownings devaluated? Was it at the Marne? At Versailles, when a new geography was being made on paper? Certainly the literary world which emerged from the war used a new coinage. In England and America the "masters" of the last century diminished in stature and pertinence, became remote and shadowy.

The final expression of this state of mind, as we have seen, is in the almost savage nostalgia of "The Old Beauty." It might not be going too far to say that in the end this increasing tendency to look backward impaired, if it did not destroy, her art. When she died in 1947 Willa Cather's contribution to American literature had long been completed.

Willa Cather

And what was the nature of that contribution? There are few writers of her distinction whose achievement is so difficult to sum up. She belongs to no school. Alfred Kazin puts her beside Ellen Glasgow as another type of "traditionalist"; Henry Seidel Canby also associates her with Ellen Glasgow in both theme and craftsmanship; Fred Millett associates her art with the "genteel realism" of Edith Wharton; Carl Van Doren contrasts her as a frontier novelist with Jack London; but the fact is that she cannot be helpfully classified with respect to either theme or technique. The heroic nostalgia that pursued her until the end first changed her from a minor imitator of James to a novelist of fierce originality and individuality, and from the moment she discovered herself with *O Pioneers!* she went her own way with remarkably little notice of her contemporaries. She developed a style both strong and supple, combining forthrightness with sensitivity: she was one of the least showy novelists of her time. Her firm conviction that, as she put it in her essay "On the Art of Fiction," "art . . . should simplify" led her to a careful precision in the choice and presentation of descriptive detail, so that her mature novels and stories are ribbed, as it were, with a solid framework of carefully selected description which becomes symbolic in virtue of its solidity and distribution.

"Any first-rate novel or story must have in it the strength of a dozen fairly good stories that have been sacrificed to it," she wrote in the same essay. Strength of this kind is to be found in most of her novels. We do not find it at all in *Alexander's Bridge* or *Lucy Gay-*

Final Estimate

heart, and we find it in *The Song of the Lark* in too great degree, so that the novel at times becomes congested; but in novels as different as *My Antonia* and *Death Comes for the Archbishop* we have a sense of power held in reserve, of the visible part of the story being only that part of the iceberg which is above the surface. The almost masculine sensibility which she displays in both these novels is an important clue to her quality as a writer.(She admired both the connoisseur and the pioneer and sought for an ideal which combined both.) Perhaps the hero of *The Professor's House* is the most revealing of all her characters, for he is both connoisseur and hero; he has a discriminating palate for sherry and a passion for the lives of great adventurers, and he flouts bourgeois standards in the name both of culture and of passionate individualism. Willa Cather did not find rugged individualism—which she admired —in the world of modern business; she found it in nineteenth-century pioneers, eighteenth-century Catholic missionaries, and seventeenth-century French Canadians. All of these in their own ways were both connoisseurs and pioneers, and she could find few of either in her own century.

Her central concern as a novelist came to be more and more that of Sir Walter Scott. Scott, too, was concerned with the fate of heroic ideals in an age of commercial progress and in his best novels presented his essentially tragic perception that progress was incompatible with the survival of the ideal of heroic action. The perception was tragic for Scott, for he wanted both; Willa Cather, as she grew older, wanted less and less of any-

187

thing the modern world could offer and so withdrew into history with fewer regrets (odd though it may seem) than the celebrated historical novelist.

Other American novelists have written about the pioneers and have gloried in their heroic qualities. But for Miss Cather heroism was not enough, and her accounts of pioneers do not simply glorify their courage and strength of purpose. She was interested in the quality of their imagination, in the passion and brilliance of their ideal, in their discriminating acceptance of a vision, as well as in their will power and endurance. The affectionate detail with which she documents the transplanting of French culture to the rock of Quebec in *Shadows on the Rock* and the subtle combination of Old World tastes and New World enthusiasms to be found among the priests in *Death Comes for the Archbishop* (one could write a whole treatise on her view of the civilizing function of the salad in old New Mexico) show clearly that she was no simple celebrator of the pioneer as such. The heroism she admires either derives from or is working toward an appropriate culture, and that culture has to be a genuine culture, a pattern of values that adds to the possibilities of discrimination as well as of zest. In many of her novels, it is the Old World that provides the discrimination and the New World that gives the zest, but it would be an oversimplification to apply this to all her work. Her feeling for Europe, like her feeling for the Cliff Dwellers, takes many forms, without ever degenerating into the simple and vulgar pursuit of an older culture. She manipulated European and American values with as much subtlety as Henry James, but with an intent wholly different from James's. Like James, however, and to an even greater degree, she remained an American novelist: she saw life in terms of the possibilities provided by the New World, and her vision darkened only when those possibilities seemed to fail.

Where to place Willa Cather finally will always puzzle the literary historians. But the reader of her best novels is not likely to worry about that. These novels have a strength and an individuality that it is not easy for the critic formally to describe, virtues which can be experienced even if they cannot easily be talked about. Her position among American novelists is unique; no other has brought to bear quite her kind of perception on the American scene. Yet the subject she handles most successfully and most characteristically— the subtilizing of courage by vision and discrimination and the search for a culture that combines all three qualities—is more than an American theme. It transcends national problems to illuminate one of the great questions about civilization. To put the matter briefly, Miss Cather's novels are civilized; and if we interpret that term too narrowly that is because we have not read Willa Cather carefully enough.

Index

Index

Index